FAUST THE DANCING CAT

TACKLES

STRIPPERS, SCAMMERS & BEARS

Signe A. Dayhoff, Ph.D.

Faust the Dancing Cat Tackles
Strippers, Scammers & Bears
by Signe A. Dayhoff, PhD

Copyright ©2017 by Signe A. Dayhoff, PhD
Published by Effectiveness-Plus Publications LLC
80 Paseo de San Antonio
Placitas, New Mexico 87043-8735

Cover design by BDT/around86 @fiverr.com
Photo ©CanStockPhoto/taden

ISBN: 978-0-9970168-7-1

DEDICATION

Faust's first book, What Faust the Dancing Cat Taught Me, detailed how I first encountered this homeless cat I named Faust who quickly became my constant companion and completely took over my life. He went everywhere with me often creating some notoriously awkward, even outrageous, situations. That was when I discovered that the expression, "Too soon old and too late smart" had become my byword with him. But I can't imagine what life would have been like in those first two years without those many feline-precipitated complications and his loving companionship.

This second book is dedicated to Faust who non-judgmentally, loyally, and lovingly continued to open up for me a wonderful, unexpected world of appreciation for inter-species communication, the vagaries and absurdities of life in general, and the overwhelming joy of having a cat companion.

It is also dedicated to all companion-animal, no-kill rescue organizations locally, nationally, and around the world, which work tirelessly, always under significantly strained financial circumstances, for homeless animals. But it is especially dedicated to Companion Animal Rescue and Medical Assistance (CARMA), Corrales, NM.

ACKNOWLEDGMENTS

This is to especially acknowledge all those of you who have known Faust in person through the years, shared his sweetness, zest for life, craziness, love, and stories, encouraged his performances, and enjoyed his antics and his ever-increasing repertoire of gymnastics. You made his life even more fun, full, and meaningful. And mine too.

This is also to acknowledge all those of you who have read and praised his first book, shared your personal cat stories with me, and clamored for more of Faust's adventures. As Faust would say, "Mohw!"—his version of "thanks."

TABLE OF CONTENTS

1

"TWILIGHT ZONE" REVISITED

Even though our unnerving nightmare had occurred more than a year ago, every now and then I found myself helplessly re-experiencing its real "cat-and-mouse" game on a dark, lonely highway. It always left me bathed in acrid sweat, my heart racing, and nerve endings snapping in the middle of the night.

Each time the dream starts out pleasantly as Faust the Dancing Cat and I are enjoying ourselves for two days at the Cranberry Hammered Dulcimer Festival at Binghamton, New York. The event is located in a church and on its grounds where we listen to well-known folk musicians playing their hammered dulcimers, mountain dulcimers, pennywhistles, and fiddles. We take a class on the physics of building a hammered dulcimer and I discover the names of those around the country who build and sell hammered dulcimers. And Faust takes it upon himself to try to play one when he's not emulating Gene Kelly for the admiring crowd.

We're there because the hammered dulcimer is a musical instrument I have wanted since I first heard it played in the theme song for PBS's original

Crockett's Victory Garden which started in Boston back in 1975. It had taken me forever to discover the name of the song, the "Gaspé Reel," who performed it, Bill Spence and Fennig's All-Star String Band, and learn everything I could about hammered dulcimers in the library. I was amazed to learn that their history went back to ancient psalteries and they were played in nearly every country under different names.

As twilight descends on Sunday, we're departing for home in Sudbury, Massachusetts. Everything starts out well, with only a medium amount of traffic sharing the road. Then when we cross from New York into Massachusetts, we find ourselves on a long isolated stretch of low-visibility, heavily-forested Massachusetts Turnpike in the western part of the state. We're about118 miles from home.

It's eerie that there's not a single other car on the road. Not having felt tired before we left, for some reason I have begun to repeatedly drift off. Each time I manage to snap back but barely in time to recover the right lane. Keeping my eyes open is a big struggle, despite several cups of coffee and a cold breeze from my driver's side window slapping me in the face. At one point I slide to the side of the road and jog around the car. It doesn't help. I have a desperate need to stop at the first rest stop we encounter to grab a quick nap. But, that desire is thwarted.

At that rest stop I discover one other car in the parking lot. It's just outside the restrooms. I wonder if its two male occupants are awaiting others who are using the facilities. The two men are eyeballing us. This makes me very uneasy. I decide to wait to see if anyone else joins them and they all leave. But no one joins them ... and they don't leave.

Time clicks by slowly. I'm still fighting heavily drooping eyelids. I want sleep so badly but they're still not leaving. They're watching me and being obvious about it. My discomfort grows more intense by the second. After twenty minutes of being observed, my fear triggers a slug of adrenaline. Suddenly my fatigue dissolves. All thoughts of sleep disappear. My eyes whip open. I throw the car into gear and pull out onto the highway. But they do the same. And they're right behind us.

Like a shadow of death, they follow closely. They mirror our every move. I change lanes. They change lanes. I speed up. They speed up. I slow down. They slow down. It's just the two of us in the middle of nowhere. I try to materialize another car—or, better yet, a state trooper—someone who would drive by, whom I could signal for assistance. But try as I may to conjure one up, no one else appears.

Even with Faust around my shoulders, I'm cold, shivering uncontrollably. For mile after mile they stalk us. My fear increases. Then, just as they close in—seemingly to ram my Rabbit's backend to run us off the road ... and do whatever—they disappear—swallowed up by the darkness at an unforeseen local exit.

Faust, my nightmare counterpart, has been my

constant companion for over two years, although sometimes it has seemed much longer. In that time together we have had many "interesting" experiences—though I'm sure he'd think of them as adventures. Some have been scary, some fun, and some just plain outlandish. In most respects, Faust often seems very human. To those who know us, we may even seem like the stereotype of an old married couple, if one member is a small, tailed, and a furry quadruped.

I encountered this gray, feline skeleton with vampire teeth in the tree-shaded gravel parking lot of the Goodnow Library in Sudbury. It was after I had given a presentation on passing the Equal Rights Amendment that he made his presence known. He oozed out from under the rear end of my car to rub against my ankles. I had never seen such a sickly, mangy-looking, cadaverous cat before. It was evident he was operating on soon-to-run-out borrowed time. However, his glinting amber eyes and gravelly version of meow, "mohw," quickly snatched my heart. I adopted him there and then, hoping I could make whatever time he had left comfortable and cared for.

But, as I was soon to learn, he had no intention of shuffling off this mortal coil any time soon. Even through multiple infections and previously damaged lungs, he would hang in there. I had had cats before but I had never had a cat like this one. From that seemingly innocuous introduction, he almost instantaneously became my alter ego and the initiator of more wild and woolly times in a few short years than I thought the average person would be likely to experience in a lifetime.

Every place I went, he went, even where and when he shouldn't. This could make even the dullest trip an exciting excursion. And, he danced. He not only danced but also performed acrobatics. Once he regained a modicum of his health and accommodated to living inside, he dumbfounded me with his desire to learn just about anything I was willing to teach him.

In fact, he initiated many of his training sessions. Often he'd show me the makings of some new behavior which he seemed to indicate he wanted me to help him refine. In many ways he was more human than cat though I suspect he would have found that analysis insulting. He appeared to view humans only slightly more intelligent than dogs with, cats, of course, perched at the pinnacle of the intelligence pecking order.

Faust would likely have been seen by outsiders as the epitome of cat independence. But while he did make many of his own decisions about what he would do—decisions which he did not want countermanded by me—in private he grudgingly acceded to my "influence" over all he did. Or, at least, he let me think so. Cats are skillful diplomats in their dealings with humans and other animals so it's hard to tell who is directing whom.

As a result of his training bent, he could do just about anything a trained dog could do ... walk on his hind legs, roll over, do back flips, catch a Wiffle

Ball in mid-air, climb a ladder, dance with flair, and "leap onto tall buildings at a single bound"—and all without the need of a red cape. Just about anything … except, of course, bark. But why would an heir to the Egyptian royal family of cats want to lower himself to do something that "brain-deficiently cacophonous" as "bark" anyway.

More than one person has laughingly suggested he was really a dog in a cat suit. It's a good thing he has never heard these comments. If he had, he would have been outraged because to him dogs mindlessly wasted many hours a day just licking their balls. Faust would acknowledge that he participated in such "licking" but *only* when it was a necessary part of his toilette. Besides, though he would have been loath to admit it, he didn't have that much left to lick after the "Great Inglorious Snip-Snip," as it was infamously referred to in the cat kingdom. He had more important, more cultural, more educational pursuits in life, such as taking every opportunity to dazzle everyday human audiences with his artistry at the slightest hint of their enlightened interest.

As that ominous dream passed, but with a lingering feeling of dread, I found I couldn't get back to sleep. Somehow I couldn't get comfortable no matter what position I tried. Of course, every little adjustment I made displaced Faust who was attempting to snuggle as close to me as possible … well, more likely attempting to reclaim more of *his* bed. From our time together it had become apparent that he had allotted me a parcel of "property" two-feet-wide and five-feet-long bordering the mattress's right edge, which, I'm sure, he thought was most generous.

It could have been worse. At least, unlike some dogs, he never tried to shove me with his back legs back to where I "belonged," or even off the bed. Instead, with god-like patience, he always chose to endure my temporarily exceeding my bounds, knowing full well he would, with careful manipulation and time, finally regain his territory. He was clearly proud of his cognitive faculties.

To remind me whose bed it really was he had a strict bed ritual. Always beginning on my pillow, he would curl around my head like an electrically-heated nightcap and lick and groom my hair. Wet hair strands would become trapped under his warm body, preventing my head movement and making my scalp feel pinched and itchy.

As I managed to extricate my hair to adjust my head and body, I'd give him more pillow room. Then I'd roll over to my left side, displacing him. He'd then automatically slide down in behind my knees, re-setting my property line: "this far but no more." Never heeding his dictates, I'd then flop onto my back signaling his imminent squishing by my thigh or being knocked senseless by my right kneecap. At this juncture he would rapidly navigate to my chest. There he'd stretch out the length of my body, with his front paws around my neck and his back legs caressing my hip bones, purring loudly, and effectively pinning me in one place.

With my last toss and turn, I would roll over to my left side again. Taking umbrage, even though he knew to expect it, he would swipe at my nose with his paw. Even without claw extension, his action would express a definite signal to me to "knock it off!"

However, if I were so foolish as to move again, as I once discovered, he would show his pique by lying on my feet, making them feel trapped and hot. That would continue until I struggled to move them, and him, which, he knew, would wake me up, and did. Cats know humans need to be trained.

The cat's moral of the story, which Faust embraced, is: "If humans want to get some uninterrupted sleep, they'd better make sure their cats can get some uninterrupted sleep *first*." Even while cats are unable—or just maybe, unwilling—to speak English, that never interferes with their ability to strongly communicate and effect their desires.

A week after that original "Twilight Zone-like" fright, I finally pulled the Louisville Slugger out from just behind my pillow, next to the headboard. It was no longer "necessary." In addition to its having created neck spasms for me, it was a definite annoyance to Faust as he endeavored to get comfortable on my pillow. Circling to lie down, he invariably knocked the wood or lay on it, causing him to have to readjust his position. I suspect he wondered why I was being so thoughtless.

But, at least, unlike many humans confronting

that situation, he politely refrained from shaking his head, rolling his eyes, or dramatically sighing. The bat soon stood leaning against the night table to the right of my bed then finally gravitated back into my clothes closet. I'm sure Faust felt he was a greater threat to be reckoned with should there be an intruder. But, like most ever-predictable humans, I tended to take too much time to recognize the obvious.

In case I missed anything in my nightly house surveillance, he had accompanied me as I checked the windows and doors before retiring. However, after a week, he seemed to tire of the routine. Alternatively, he chose to sit in the doorways between rooms to supervise my robotic activity, no doubt thinking, "How has this irrational human species managed to survive this long?"

Faust enjoyed our trips together, especially those that were extended—"extended" for him was anything outside Sudbury and taking more than a day. He was looking forward to another one coming up soon. We hadn't taken one in over a year which left Faust antsy. As a result, he was impatiently waiting. As the time dragged on, he began to pace by the kitchen door to the garage. To remind me he pawed the doorjamb, without claws, looking back at me to make sure he had gotten my attention. If I didn't respond immediately, he would jump to grab hold of the door knob and nonchalantly swing there until it opened ... or I removed him.

Given his already feeling trip-deprived, I

regretted having to inform him that we wouldn't be traveling across country as soon as I had previously suggested we would. I'd promised that we'd tour the western National Parks in a month or so but now I had things to do before we could go. Therefore, we wouldn't be likely to go any sooner than a year from next June. As it turned out, even though Faust did not know it yet, he would have lots to keep him busy until then.

2

FAUST TAKES B.U. BY STORM

Since Binghamton, over two years had passed during which I had added another degree to my résumé. My first two graduate degrees had been in English and Psychology. Until I was certain what I really wanted to do next, I had continued my freelance writing, editing, and marketing communications work. I also had had two books on alternative approaches to career development published by a smaller press, Brick House, in Acton, Massachusetts.

Occasionally, I taught at Framingham South High School as a substitute in English. I instructed in grammar, composition, and literature. This was not my favorite activity because it was at a time when students were just being allowed to feel their independence as individuals. This is in spite of the fact that children at that age were less able to successfully handle such unfettered freedom. As a consequence of being nearly unrestrained, they would demonstrate a newly-acquired sense of rebellion by talking back to me or doing disruptive things in class while I was attempting to convey some subject-relevant information.

Principals likewise had decided in this new era of more laissez-faire treatment of students that sending the unruly ones to the office was no longer acceptable. We teachers were expected to "deal" with it ourselves. I was most definitely not amused. Despite being non-violent (except for when the vulnerable needed protecting), I had a low tolerance for teenagers being totally obnoxious as they attempted to push the envelope beyond all recognition. To my shame I fantasized more than once about taking control by slamming some insufferable little miscreant against a locker for what he had said or done.

As a sub, I had no power, having had little time to develop a bond with students. But teachers in general had had their power and influence reduced significantly. From my perspective it was not a healthy or effective educational situation. At least the substitute-teaching and my freelance writing together paid enough to keep me in crackers and peanut butter as I wrestled with what I wanted to do next. My greatest fear was becoming a "bag lady."

As much as I enjoyed the writing aspects of my communications work, and doing my work nationally, I was tired of doing technical brochures. Brochures, in all shapes and sizes, could be about nearly anything—from the electronics of submersible equipment to surgical eye ointment— and could incorporate any number of photos, illustrations, graphs, lists, as well as text in slick folders.

All marketing pieces and articles were to highlight what the company or organization provided, how it matched with the audience's needs and desires, and attempted to tickle and entice the public or the organization's clients to use the company's service and/or products. These were inevitably subjects about which I knew very little at first glance. Fortunately I was good at research, a fast learner, and managed to capture what the companies wanted and do it on schedule.

Regarding getting my work done, Faust always became involved and rendered his "assistance." That is, he would frequently sit directly on documents over which I was slaving. This could be someone else's manuscript I was editing, a brochure I was creating, or an article I was writing. He was my "proofreader." That is, he would rectally scan these documents for errors for me. While his proofreading was an important and helpful skill, the fact that he couldn't communicate what he had read tended to slow my progress. However, to be fair, at times his assistance with a troublesome piece often provided me with a much needed a break … and a good laugh.

Other people's book manuscripts became the bane of my existence. But it wasn't all book manuscripts. It was primarily the manuscripts of first-time writers. Neophytes understandably viewed their compositions as sacrosanct—untouchable—while experienced writers were eager for any suggestions from an objective grammar-and-composition eye to improve their works.

As a result, even though new writers would hire me to edit and make relevant, useful suggestions, emotional clashes were likely to occur. This is because they tended to become extremely indignant at any notation I made or suggestion I wrote on or about their literary "baby." They didn't seem to comprehend, even though we would discuss the project at length ahead of time, the need for these notations to be on the manuscript page itself. Most had to be directly tied to the word, phrase, or concept in question. To be listed on a separate sheet *only*—where fuller explanations and comments were also written—would not be pragmatic, as quickly and easily understandable, or as helpful.

Conflicts usually started with defensive questions: "Why did you do that? What do you mean there's a problem with syntax? What's syntax? What difference does it make? I know what I mean. What's wrong with '... as infrequent as a female fowl's dental implants'? Why can't you say, 'The chocolate cupcake was fraught with vanilla cream'? You're being too picky. The readers will know what I mean. What do you mean it 'rambles and needs to be tighter' or needs to be expressed in different ways? All that information is absolutely essential as it is."

Next were the challenges to my comprehension of what they had written: "What do you mean it doesn't sound 'realistic'? You weren't there; I was. That's exactly the way it happened." They didn't seem to realize that even though *they* had experienced whatever-it-was, their writing didn't quite put their readers smack-dab in the situation to experience it for themselves. They needed to become aware of how and why they had responded to the situation so they could convey that sense of intimacy and immediacy to their readers.

And finally there were what infrequently became preliminary to threats of non-payment as a result of everything I had done, as per their instructions: "You've made this manuscript mess. It was clean and now it has notes and marks all over the place. You've ruined it. How can I send it out to anyone as it is? Now I have to retype the whole thing. This isn't what I wanted you to do—what I asked you to do. You evidently have no idea what you're doing. Do you really expect me to pay for *this*?" This was usually followed by attempts at shaking the hundreds of carefully edited, double-spaced pages in my face.

Faust, who was invariably present when I met these clients, sat on my desk, watching closely. As the client's strained voice rose, Faust's eyes were reduced to knife slits, his every muscle coiled and poised as if ready to spring like a jaguar, if necessary, at this attacking person. It was unheard of for him to growl to show his displeasure. He only stared, ears back, his slim face drawn into a taut mask of disapproval. But it was usually sufficiently disconcerting to those complaining that after I went through the agreed-upon details of their contract again, they quickly folded up their tents and stole off into the night, no doubt, still unhappy and disbelieving. Despite their complaints, it was rare I had to take them to small claims court.

As soon as they left, Faust would be bunting my chest with his head and licking my face. Patiently he awaited his much-deserved kitty treat reward for running interference for me. As Faust would concur, size doesn't matter. It's what you do with it.

Being business-like, I always used detailed, carefully spelled out, signed contracts with clients which we discussed at length so we were, hopefully, on the same page about precisely what they *said* they wanted me to do and what I agreed to do for them. Even though they had their copy of this agreement, too often when their blood-and-tears new literary effort was the object of contention, the client's memory, rationality, emotion, and surging adrenaline didn't always coincide.

When I could step back to view these conflicts more objectively, I found it was the psychology of the interactions that always lassoed me and dragged me in to observe it. In fact, that interest seemed to be calling to me, tugging on my passion's sleeve. I wondered why people responded as they did and what thoughts, feelings, beliefs, attitudes, history, and associations influenced their behavior. But determining what area of psychology I wanted to pursue was weighing me down.

My Master's degree in psychology had been an amalgam of social, educational, and clinical psychology. However, the more disagreements I had to deal with unraveling and explaining the writing problems of some of my editing clients, the more I gravitated toward social psychology. As a result, two years previously I had applied to Boston University for their Social Psychology PhD Program, been accepted, and was finally getting close to finishing.

What particularly appealed to me about social psychology was that it deals with humans' interactions with other humans and with the environment, the effects of those interactions, why and how they take place, and their likely meanings given the circumstances and contexts. Even though Faust was not a "real" human, I could see his desires and behaviors paralleling those of humans in general and mine in particular. While he couldn't express his attitudes, emotions, and attributions to what caused things to happen or his goals in words, he could demonstrate how he felt, what he wanted in interacting with me and the world, and the effect of his achieving his goals.

Boston University had been of particular interest because of the applied, as opposed to basic, research emphasis of their program. Moreover, at that time, once one received a doctorate in social psychology, she or he could then slide directly into their Clinical Psychology PhD Program. Learning more about applying cognitive-behavioral principles was likewise a goal of mine. Over my time at B.U., Faust remained my constant companion, joining me—if not in classes I took, than in my office and in the classes I taught.

On a teaching fellowship, I taught General

Psychology to the Liberal Arts and Sciences students and to the Fine Arts students. These classes of students were as different as White Castle hamburger is to Maxims-de-Paris's filet mignon. The Liberal Arts freshmen seemed like bored children, wanting to be elsewhere but being forced to attend this required class. They rarely asked questions or offered relevant comments, too often, instead, whispering to one another or reading something other than the textbook. This was a challenge I wasn't sure how to master. I'd hate to think what that classroom would have been like if this had been the era of the cell phone or iPhone. Still I felt like Dorothy uncomfortably repeating, "Lions and tigers and bears, oh my!"

During the first class with Liberal Arts students, Faust was present, observing. When I introduced him, I intended to have him demonstrate some fun psychological principles, such as how to influence or condition various behaviors in animals and humans, a subject I thought would capture their interest. But it never happened. Just being present, Faust gave the students an excuse—as if they needed one—to be rowdy, calling to him, making "meow" sounds. The noise and commotion made Faust confused and anxious.

As a student instructor without the benefit of respected title and any real clout, like a high school substitute teacher, I felt impotent to bring order quickly to the nearly one hundred students seated on wooden bleachers in the large classroom. Squirming out of my arms, Faust desperately tried to escape into his closed carrier, to hunker down in a corner, facing away from the dissonant chaos. If only they had allowed him, he would have been delighted to dance for them and give them a taste of how he had learned to accomplish his many tricks—excuse me, I mean "performance art." However, after their less than respectful greetings, he seemed happier—well, less unhappy—staying in my office during those specific classes.

Not knowing how the Fine Arts freshmen would react, I decided to cautiously try again. If only there were a way I could check them out without their making Faust so agitated. Was he willing to try again? When I asked him as he sat on my old wooden office desk, he looked at me curiously, ears back slightly, tail rhythmically swishing. "You don't have to go," I reminded him. "But if you don't, you'll have to stay here in the office and find something else to do."

Unfortunately I couldn't provide him with a deck of cards, a crossword puzzle, a Rubik's Cube, or book to read if he stayed behind. Not having opposable thumbs made some activities difficult for him. I was sure he was more than a little cognizant of that fact, thank you very much. However, when I added, "If they'd welcome your presence," he looked at me, his ears came forward a little, and his tail stopped. I had his attention. "Then you'd get a chance to show off for them your many skills, such as your illustrious Viennese waltz technique. You know they'd enjoy that." Faust opened his eyes wide and reached his front legs to caress my neck.

"Okay, you ham, let's go check it out. But just in case, keep all your paws crossed it will work."

For this first class Faust was in his carrier instead of lounging around my neck as he normally rode with me on campus. It was a long walk to this new classroom. We had to traverse the distance from my office in the two-story brick building at 64 Cummington Street, across railroad tracks, to 685 Commonwealth Avenue then travel northwest to the Metropolitan College Building at 755. Because of the traffic, noise, and glut of pedestrians passing us in both directions, I didn't want Faust exposed to it all, unprotected. I was concerned about his emotional state when we finally arrived.

Our current destination was a first floor room, inside the front door to the left, where the class was being held temporarily. When we reached the small room, twenty students were likewise arriving in twos and threes. Inside the door was a grand piano, angled in front of a long blackboard. Since chalk was always being surreptitiously lifted by desperate instructors, I had to bring my own just in case. This was one of the things no one tells a new instructor. On my first day of teaching, with the Liberal Arts students, I had been incredibly lucky to find a sliver the size of a pencil eraser. What remained when I finished the class I left, though I doubt anyone could have written with it.

I placed Faust's carrier on the closed lid of the piano as I greeted the students. Once they were assembled, I introduced myself with a big smile, purposely leaving Faust out for a moment. Their curiosity about the carrier was palpable. As they finished seating themselves, I said, "Oh, by the way, I thought you might like to meet Faust."

Lifting him out of his carrier, I placed him on the piano lid. "This is the famous feline, Faust the Dancing Cat." He seemed to nod his head in a bow of humility. Their reaction was gratifying. I heard, "Hello, Faust, Glad you could join us." "Will *you* be teaching a lesson today?" I had to grin with gratitude at their level of civility for eighteen year olds.

Calmly sitting on the piano, Faust seemed comfortable and involved. He raised his whiskers into his vampire smile which resulted in some soft chuckles from the students. Surprisingly, and thoughtfully, he stayed where he was instead of wandering over to the keyboard to try to tickle the ivories or hop down to visit the room's occupants one by one, as he, an esteemed social cat, was wont to do.

I explained, "Faust will be joining us often to participate in demonstrations of various psychological principles. This is not going to be a course about facts for the sake of remembering rote facts. You live psychology and need to know how it explains who you are, your thoughts and feelings, attitudes and beliefs, what influences your thoughts, relationships, and goals, as well as what you do, why you do it, and under what conditions … from the inside out.

"What that means is we'll talk about such topics as neurophysiology, cognitive-behavior therapy, social anxiety, sexual attraction, how different cultures show the same emotional expressions, how societies differ in their concepts of what is beautiful, how and why we tend to relate to non-human animals, ... and so much more. This will be a course of using your own experiences to discover and understand how and why you act and relate as you do and why others, likewise, act as they do.

"One of the psychological principles Faust will demonstrate in class is the behavioral concept of 'shaping.' Shaping is where one takes an existing natural behavior in an animal or human and modifies it slowly and incrementally, through successive approximations of the final behavior, using positive reinforcement, where each step gets you closer to the desired new behavior."

As I placed the carrier on the piano bench, I said, "Let me give you an idea of what Faust will be showing you. It's one example of this shaping method. I'm sure you all know the Strauss's 'Blue Danube Waltz.' On the count of three I want you all to start to hum it in the key of D." I hummed the note. "One, two, three ..."

As we collectively hummed, I looked at Faust, secured his attention, and rotated my hand. On cue, he stood on his hind legs and began to turn around in a circle on the piano top, stepping, dipping, and swaying in time to his human accompaniment. After fifteen seconds, he was moving precipitously close to the lid edge. I was about to stop him to prevent his falling but his audience did it for me ... with their applause.

He stopped. Immediately he sat down facing them, his ears forward, his whiskers raised again, pleased with himself and soaking up their adulation. Later in the semester when we talked at length about behavioral psychology and conditioning, Faust kindly would lie on the floor so I could demonstrate how he had been conditioned to roll over on cue. That would segue into a discussion of how the same principles could be applied to change humans' behavior as well.

In every class with the Fine Arts students, he sat quietly on the piano until I requested his participation. It was going really well. That is, until one morning. I was explaining a perceptual phenomenon, or optical illusion, resulting from spinning a color wheel. Faust had experienced the motor and whirling disk before so he took the movement, whirring sound, and generated airflow in stride. If only the color wheel could have been as accommodating.

Constructed of paperboard, which is slightly heavier than cardstock, this color wheel had undoubtedly been created in some past century and now suffered from severe material fatigue. It was composed of seven wedges of different colors. I could see that the hole in the cardboard that fitted over the rotating axle of the motor was slightly enlarged from use but hadn't given it much thought. Putting it in place and switching on the motor, I asked, "Can you still see all the colors?" They shook their heads. "What do you see instead?" "White," they responded. "Why do you see the colors change to white as the wheel rotates?"

Suddenly the wheel exploded. More precisely, the cardboard disintegrated. Fibrous pieces flew in every direction. Faust sprang high into the air with a stifled mohw. A red piece struck me low on the forehead. It knocked off my glasses and drew blood. As Faust landed back on the piano lid, his body swiped the still-whirling mechanism. With a slap he tossed it onto the floor where it rat-a-tat-a-tatted. In the meantime, as the world seemed to darken around me, I folded myself onto the piano bench, beside his carrier, with my head down.

Faust jumped off the piano. Perhaps, I struggled to think straight, it was to retrieve the offending piece of cardboard for me. But more likely it was to find the nearest outside door to crawl under. As students started to rush toward me to make sure I was all right, he was cringing against the door jamb. He looked in the throes of stultifying panic, as if a Bull Mastiff were hunkered over him, planning his evisceration, his demise imminent. But then, as the horde converged on me, he suddenly reversed himself.

Immediately he hurdled over the bench onto the piano keyboard, slamming the eighth octave high C key and the B below it. His long thin gray tail fuzzed out and back arched, he stood in front of me. I was still sitting slouched over it, my left hand on the piano's top edge for balance. Scrutinizing the concerned crowd, Faust seemed to be daring them to do anything untoward to his best friend. His behavior practically spelled out in fluorescent letters three feet high: "No you don't! Not on my watch!"

The students quickly recognized his protective move and simultaneously broke into applause again. This thoroughly confused poor Faust. He seemed unsure. Were they authentically praising him for his bold actions? Or were they were trying to distract him from his sworn duty in order to attack me?

Still feeling a little out of kilter from the concussive blow, and in need of a Band-Aid, I dismissed the class early. As Faust relaxed, he climbed onto my shoulders and curled his body around my neck. The concerned students who were filing past handed me my glasses, which had been sent to the floor, and asked if I needed a glass of water or help getting back to my office. One by one they reached to give Faust a well-deserved pat on the head or a scratch under his chin. Being a magnanimous feline, he accepted their "Well done!" honoraria, his amber eyes gleaming at their attention. One theater major, who always came into class with unusual grease paint designs on her face, perhaps trying to "shock" me, reached around Faust to give me a half-hug. Faust stiffened, sniffed her face, wrinkled his nose ... and sneezed.

Classes with the Fine Arts first-year students, who represented the School of Music, the School of Theatre, and the School of Visual Arts, were always enjoyable, always stimulating for me and, I think, for them too. They acted like adults who appeared attuned, disciplined, and interested. What I soon discovered as I queried them and attempted to arouse their curiosity was that they took notes, asked prescient questions, responded to my prompts, and contributed to the class. They seemed to absorb all they could, while weighing how the information could be applied to their lives and artistic focus. Those were the students who took advantage of my office hours.

The music students especially seemed more mature in their attitudes and approach. They knew precisely what was required of them, that to do it right took time, effort, and dedication. This world view and achievement orientation evidently applied to everything they did. They reminded me of music students I'd known at Baylor University, where I'd started college, like violinist Pamela Pandolfi whom I admired.

Starting at the age of four to study the violin, Pam became a soloist with the Greenville Symphony Orchestra and went on to found the well-known Cary School of Music in Cary, North Carolina, in 1993, a school which provides an easily accessible, affordable, attractive, and joyful environment for the study and performance of music. Music students, especially, were people who knew they were going someplace and were assiduously preparing for it. Working with them was like being on another planet by comparison with the Liberal Arts students.

Only one Fine Arts student didn't appear to fit in with his compatriots. He sat quietly in class, slouched down in his seat. He didn't seem to relate to Faust or show any interest in anything we discussed. He acted as if he were invisible even when I gently tried to involve him. When the assignment was to do a simple psychological study based on detailed, straightforward observation, he handed in a graded paper from another course. I spoke with him after class to determine why this had happened, but he said nothing. He offered no excuse, no defense.

I asked, "Would it be helpful if I went over what you needed to do for the assignment? If it isn't clear or you feel unsure or confused, I could further clarify it." He didn't respond. "Do you have any questions?" He shook his head.

At that point I indicated that the other course's paper he had submitted merited an "F" in this class. "If you were to actually do the assignment and hand it by the end of next week, I'd grade it. However, in fairness to the other students who did it and did it on time, I'd have to reduce your paper one grade for being late. So if you turned in an 'A' paper, you'd receive a 'B.' That would be lots better than the current 'F.'"

He nodded as if he understood. However, the next class he was a no-show. He never reappeared and, sadly, received "F" for the entire course, unless the administration was willing to expunge it for some reason. I didn't like to give that kind of demoralizing course grade but he had left me no choice. His actions suggested that there was some difficulty with which he was unsuccessfully dealing—something he wasn't about to share with me.

I wished all my teaching classes could have been with the Fine Arts people because they brought out the best in me and I felt I reciprocated. Of course, Faust's presence made everything even better. At the same time, I also knew I had failed the Liberal Arts students who, as a mass, seemed alienated, anonymous, and unfocused. I struggled to get beyond their seemingly dismissive group attitude in class to give them, as a whole, my best. But, sadly, I never felt I did so completely.

At least in each of the smaller Liberal Arts' discussion groups—about fifteen students per— gratifyingly we made considerable progress through asking and answering questions. My objective was to stimulate them to think critically and question everything. I didn't invite Faust to attend because I feared he'd be a distraction.

We watched films, discussed various theories in areas of psychological research and how they applied to their lives. I challenged their ideas and we did thought experiments. Over time, that mutual success made trying to teach their large class a little less onerous. I hoped that by getting to interact with me on a more personal basis and doing activities that were better suited to small groups than to large ones, they were better able to see how the course could be useful.

3

WHAT COLOR WAS MY PARACHUTE?

My doctoral research was on the effects of mentoring and networking on achieving work advancement. Over the years I had noticed that the kind of social interaction individuals had at work and what they did with it appeared to make a big difference in their overall success and upward mobility. The social interaction could be classified as *informal*, achieved through networks of people, and *formal*, achieved through an individual mentor.

Mentors were generally at least one step above the individual be mentored—not the person's supervisor—and possessed some status and influence. I wondered which interactions—with informal and/or formal information access and assistance—and what interaction circumstances were the most effective for providing the resources necessary for organizational advancement.

Through a series of large-scale studies with business people, males and females, who ranged in age from 23 to 59, and who represented different social, racial, ethnic, and economic backgrounds, I looked at what conditions made career development and advancement most likely. To make the findings most useful for application, the business people were not asked what they *thought they would do* but, instead, were put into situations to see what they *actually would do.*

Alas, Faust was not allowed to be present for fear of distracting participants and negatively influencing the results. Any time he was presented with an audience, he would perform his heart out. His mantra, borrowed from *The Mary Tyler Moore Show* episode "Chuckles Bites the Dust," was "a little song, a little dance, a little seltzer down your pants." As a result, while I was conducting those experiments, he had a lot of office time which seemed to bore and frustrate him.

As soon as I returned to my office, he would make these pathetic whimpering sounds, as if to further add to my guilt for leaving him alone. "Faust," I teased, "I could buy some Berlitz language records so you could learn conversational Russian, Mandarin, or Hindi in case we travel internationally. You'd have one-on-one tutoring in the privacy of my office while I'm gone. Wouldn't that be great?" He cocked his head to the right and just eyed me, as if he couldn't believe a human—*his* human—could be so dumb. Being multi-lingual was not one of his cat goals. It was obvious he thought I should have picked up on that after all this time. Then he put his head down, looked up at me scornfully, lifted a front paw, licked it, and washed his face. Sometimes it seemed he couldn't take a joke.

What I discovered in my research was that both mentoring and networking were essential for achieving success and advancement in an organization but in different and very specific ways. If you wanted to advance, the best approach was for you to have four *impersonal* contacts (via a network) within the organization who could provide you with informational resources AND only one *personal* contact (via a mentor) within the organization who could provide you with emotional support, inside information, coaching, advice, and influence.

The degree of visibility of your network and mentor was extremely important. Your *impersonal* network contacts should be high-visibility because it showed that you were taking advantage of what was commonly available. Your seeking out these instrumental resources was seen positively by everyone. Moreover, everyone could have access to this kind of information if they sought it. However, your *personal* mentor contact should be low-visibility because not everyone could easily have access to a mentor within the organization.

Mentors at that time generally chose those people whom they would mentor. If it were widely known that you alone had been singled out to have this special help by an influential other, it could cause envy among peers who didn't have this kind of access. The result could easily have a negative effect on your work environment, successful endeavors, advancement, and your career. These research findings were the first time that the numbers and visibility of necessary resources were found to be such important factors in how likely individuals were to advance in their organizations.

After I had finished my dissertation in May, I met with my committee for the two-hour defense of it. Thankfully, my work was approved. I was feeling exhausted after weeks of all-nighters checking analyses and re-writing the dissertation, relieved, and strangely a little lackadaisical. Faust, who had been forbidden to attend my defense and had to stay, once again, in my five-by-eight office, begged to be let out. And why not let him? Most everyone had already left for the summer so I was comfortable giving his curiosity free rein for a few minutes before we headed home. Cats need to explore and discover.

The second floor of the Psychology Department, the location of my closet-like cubicle, appeared to be vacant. As I gathered all my remaining papers and belongings, Faust began to wander the hall, trying to peer into doorways, most of which were closed and locked, sniffing the gray linoleum floor for any experimental white mouse that might have escaped its maze. He was to be disappointed on that score.

Suddenly, a terrorized squeal echoed through the hallway. "Oh, my god!" I gasped. "Faust, Are you okay?"

Dropping my briefcase on the floor, I tore out of my office. I didn't know which way to go. Then I heard something ... like moaning. I started in that direction. The sound drew me to the office of one of my associate professors. The door was ajar with Faust standing just inside it. He was inquisitively watching the woman who was behind her desk, hyperventilating. "It's a cat!" she squeaked. "I'm deathly afraid of cats! Take it away."

"I'm so sorry," I apologized profusely. "I had no idea anyone was still here." Lifting Faust into my arms, I continued to speak slowly, calmly to her. Sharing how my mother had at one time feared cats until she was given one as a pet that loved her unconditionally, I moved infinitesimally closer to her desk. Even though she was breathing more normally now, her face was still slightly contorted, eyes wide, and her mouth open as if ready to scream again.

I asked, "Would you like to meet Faust? He really loves people."

She shook her head, without taking her attention off him.

"Would you be willing to close your eyes, put out your hand, and let Faust rub against it? He's very sorry he startled you and really wants to apologize."

She seemed to roll that around in her mind for a minute. Hesitatingly, she put her hand out, closed her eyes, and turned her head and upper body away. I stepped closer. Just as she was about to touch Faust's soft short gray fur, there was a sound in the hallway.

She looked startled and then embarrassed and quickly withdrew her hand. "No," she started to breathe faster again, "I don't think so."

"I'm sorry about startling you but I want you to know I've enjoyed working with you. You've been very kind and helped me a great deal."

She nodded. I smiled, turned around, and left with Faust still in my arms. He seemed to have quickly gotten beyond her initial fear emanations but looked a bit perplexed. I could see him wondering why she had responded to him like that. That wasn't how most people responded to him. They were glad to see him. They didn't make frightening noises.

My mouth was dry so I stopped at a water fountain in the hall to get a drink. When I finished, I looked around, saw no one, and tapped the top of the fountain. Faust jumped out of my arms onto it. I pushed the water release button and he slurped as the water made a small arc in front of him, droplets clinging to his whiskers and fur. Back in my office he stayed seated on my straight-backed wooden chair, repeatedly wiping the excess water from his face with his licked front paw.

As soon as I had all my papers together in my briefcase and had stowed his cleaned out water and food dishes and temporary litter box into a large, handled paper bag, I placed him into his carrier which had been parked on the floor in the corner. Feeling like a pack mule hauling my three cumbersome bundles, I waddled down the stairs, swaying from railing to railing, and out to my car in the parking garage across the street.

May commencement was held under the right-side arches of Marsh Chapel on campus on Commonwealth Avenue. In the shade of the colonnade, there were arranged two columns of five gray steel folding chairs per row for five rows for graduates, in front, and guests, in back. At the front there was a dais, lectern with microphone, and a small table with carefully rolled parchment-looking diplomas wrapped with a single, narrow, red satin ribbon.

Fortunately no one questioned me when I brought Faust to my graduation. Though, perhaps, I should have questioned it myself. I suspect no one had challenged me because his small carrier was somewhat obscured by my commencement gown. It was a flowing, nearly floor-length garment of maroon polyester-cotton mix with black velvet draping. I felt more than a bit awkward wearing such fancy ritual attire, even if only for an hour or so. The gown itself had fluting around the shoulders and lantern sleeves with black velvet piping around the cuffs. A hidden zipper ran up the back. Black velvet curved around the throat and down the front. Topping off the gown was a black velvet tam with a gold metallic tassel which was to be worn on the right side before graduation.

I'm not much for this kind of ceremony. In fact, I had skipped graduations for my two Masters degrees. Despite what my advisors had urged back then, I made up excuses for non-attendance and requested they mail me the diplomas. Social anxiety reared its ugly head when I was on display in public, specifically when I was not actually doing something. Giving a presentation, teaching, or acting in a play was different. I wasn't just standing there with my face hanging out. But my absence from this ceremony wasn't going to work.

My advisor, one of the founders of the National Training Laboratories for human relations and organizational dynamics, psychologist Dr. Robert Chin, would hear none of it. Since he planned to retire soon, he wanted me to provide representation and recognition for his work with me here and now as his final successful dissertation student.

As commencement unfolded, there were addresses by Dean Geoffrey Bannister and President John Silber. As they began, surreptitiously I slipped Faust out of his carrier, which was parked under my chair, onto my lap. He sat quietly, looking around, shedding his short gray fur onto the black velvet front of my gown. Sometimes it seemed that it didn't matter how much I brushed him. And today, for whatever reason, he was graciously "sharing" a lot of his hair with me, at a most inauspicious time. Making matters more problematic, with all the stress of the day I had forgotten to bring an adhesive roller to remove cat hair. You can remove only so much cat hair with a little spit on your fingers.

As Drs. Silber and Bannister finally began to call the graduates' names alphabetically, I opened the carrier's front steel grid door in order to place Faust back inside. But Faust had other ideas. He was content to look around, feel the warm breezes, and be part of the festivities. Return to his carrier? I don't think so. If only I'd had had a carrier that had a top opening as well. If someone actually manufactured this boon to cat-mom-kind at this time, I was totally unaware of it.

Faust squirmed. The more I pushed, the more spread-eagle his legs became. Doubled over, with my hands between my legs, I tried to grab his front and back paws. My hands kept getting stuck in the folds of my gown. He made a rumbling sound. Graduates seated on both sides of me looked askance, simultaneously surprised by his presence. Their shocked expressions whispered, "Don't you *dare* mess up my big day!" Embarrassed, I half-grinned and gave Faust a final push. He responded with a low, disgruntled mohw. A few heads turned. I beseeched the heavens to let the earth open up and swallow us both ... now!

No sooner had I gotten Faust restrained than I was next in line to be called. My heart cannonading loudly enough for all to hear, I slipped out of my seat and walked unsteadily down the aisle. President Silber congratulated me. Then Dean Bannister handed me my diploma with his left hand and simultaneously shook my right hand underneath the diploma. It's a good thing he began his movements a nanosecond before I had to respond because my mind had gone completely blank.

Sweat was soaking me under my gown despite

the seventy-two-degree temperature this glorious spring day. For only a second I stood there, face red, and looked at the assembled. I saw a few smiles and thumbs-up from my doctoral colleagues. I managed a tentative smile back. Somehow—though I don't know how—my mind clicked back to the situation at hand. Thankfully, I deftly moved my tam's tassel from the right side to the left. Now that I'd made it all ritualistically "legal" I could return to my seat. And I had managed not to humiliate myself in the process.

As the procession of graduates getting their paper was completed, I pulled Faust out again. I felt guilty about having to forcefully cage him. At first he sat quietly on my lap, ignoring my petting. He was getting his annoyance across. Then he spotted my tassel and began to bat it. "Good grief, Faust! No!" I whispered harshly. "I have to return this rental ... once I get all your cat hair off ... so don't make it worse."

His ears back and his nose out of joint, he settled back on my lap, not looking at me. Still I was very glad he had been there with me. But I was even happier that he hadn't interfered with the ceremony. I had taken a big chance. He was a great guy, but he was also a cat.

After graduation, instead of signing up for B.U.'s Clinical Psychology PhD Program, I signed up for a Master's program in counseling at another institution. Unfortunately, as I finished my social psychology degree, the powers-that-be had decided that the option of going directly into the clinical doctoral program from social psychology was no longer going to be available. I later heard that a couple of the top clinical people in the program were either going elsewhere or shifting their research focus. So, the only alternative was switching colleges and programs. I went full-time, starting that summer, working nights, and finished the counseling program in slightly over a year, much of the time taken up by an internship.

By then it was definitely time for Faust and me to take a trip. We badly needed a vacation. But it wouldn't be the cross-country trip I had envisioned for us just yet. That had to be put off indefinitely because I had a new career to work on and get up to speed. The transition would take time and wouldn't be easy, especially financially. I was moving from writing, editing, and marketing consulting to coaching social effectiveness (overcoming obstacles, eliminating limiting beliefs, and increasing confidence) for individuals and providing seminars on networking and mentoring for businesspeople. But, irrespective, first we had to have a well-deserved, albeit short, break.

4

PIT AND THE PENDULUM

Our trip was going to be something like the old Bing Crosby-Bob Hope 1942 comedy film, "Road to Morocco," except Faust and I weren't two fast-talking guys castaway on a desert shore who were going to be sold into slavery to a beautiful princess. We would encounter lots of sand but no freighters, explosions, spitting camels, wielded scimitars, diaphanously-draped Dorothy Lamour, or the mellifluous-crooning of Crosby.

Our "Morocco" was the unique Desert of Maine, the forty-acre tract of exposed glacial silt in barren dunes that was surrounded by a pine forest and vegetation, near Freeport, the home of L.L. Bean. Because it received an abundance of precipitation, it wasn't a true desert. It just looked that way. Now preserved as a natural curiosity, with a gift shop and a farm museum, the Desert of Maine had originated when a family named Tuttle had purchased the land to farm in 1797. But land clearance, sheep over-grazing, and failure to rotate crops led to soil erosion. The erosion exposed the sand-like glacial silt which spread and ultimately took over the entire farm. The land was abandoned, sold, and finally converted into a tourist attraction in 1925.

When I mentioned our proposed trip to a friend who was editor of a local Boston magazine, she asked if I'd record our adventures, sort of as a humorous travel-with-pet column à la Steinbeck's *Travels With Charley,* for an edition to come out in five or six months. Why not, I thought, even though that elevated description of our adventure-to-be was asking a lot. Faust was hardly a poodle riding in a truck pulling a camper. Somehow driving in my chartreuse VW Rabbit, without camping gear, and staying in a bucolic motel didn't have the same flair.

I didn't share with Faust that canine comparison given his general attitude about the intelligence of dogs. Though I suspect he viewed poodles as a cut above—certainly not on the level with cats—but possessing a little more gray matter than the average canine. Well, that was except when they were given their "stylish" fur trims. Faust rarely seemed to approve of naked canine flesh surrounded by undignified softball-size spheres of puffy fur. Whenever he encountered the neighbor's standard poodle, Gracie, whose fur was left au natural, he seemed to half-heartedly accept the dog as sharing his street.

Before we could start our trip, I wanted the Rabbit to have a tune-up. I normally checked the oil and transmission fluid levels and replaced whatever was needed. I had replaced spark plugs when necessary and re-inflated temperature-change-induced low-pressure tires. I had changed tires on desolate roads, once in the pouring rain. On really bitter-temperature mornings I had used jumper cables and a neighbor's car to jump-start my engine.

However, even given all my basic car maintenance knowledge, I had great difficulty changing the oil filter. One factor was the height of the Rabbit from the ground. The car was so low that I needed either a hydraulic lift or jack stands in order to get under the chassis to reach the filter to do it. The other factor was being physically able to un-torque a filter that had been firmly screwed in place by the manufacturer.

Several years after purchasing the Rabbit, I had carefully rolled the car onto some jack stands I'd purchased from Lowe's. Underneath the oil filter, I placed the triangular dirty-oil receptacle. Scooting under the car on my back on an old, frayed chocolate-brown bath towel, I tried using a large, heavy pipe wrench on the filter. It seemed to weigh a ton as I finagled it over my face, attempting to get traction from the side. No matter how I tried to level or angle the wrench, I couldn't get a good grip. Moreover, I risked deforming the filter ... and worse, hitting myself in the face, breaking my glasses, and removing my front teeth. Forget thumb-tight. This filter was practically welded on.

Scooting out from under the car, rolling the towel with me, I rummaged around in the tool box in the Sudbury one-car garage. The only other wrench available was a channel lock. Surprisingly, it fitted around the filter, gripping it substantially, but the filter still wouldn't budge.

How much torque did it need? Would changing my position relative to the filter help? Re-setting the towel, I crawled under the filter and tugged and tugged for more than five minutes, enlarging my biceps but cramping my right shoulder. Then I heard something. Suddenly, the filter let loose. In an instant, my face, glasses, hair, and shirt were bathed in brown viscosity. Shocked and momentarily blinded, I tried to hurriedly move out of the way, bumping my head on the undercarriage. I barely managed to shift the oil receptacle underneath the oil stream before the filter emptied totally. Facepalm. Kee-rap!

Three showers later I still wasn't sure I had gotten all the oil out of every upper-body crevice, and especially out of my hair. I was certain I was turning my hair into straw from the repeated shampoo-ings, no matter what the Breck Shampoo Company claimed through their beautiful illustrations of models with gorgeous hair who allegedly used their product: Cheryl Tiegs, Cybille Shepherd, Jacklyn Smith, Brooke Shields, Farrah Fawcett, and Christie Brinkley. But, the real question was, had any of them every bathed their manes in molasses-like motor oil before shampooing?

My clothing had had to be coated in cornstarch, scrubbed with a nail brush, soaked in dish washing detergent, scrubbed mercilessly again, rinsed in vinegar, and finally dumped into the washing machine. I swear I could still see the stains multiple washings later. The fabric also suffered appreciably under all that wear and tear. As much as I felt like a wimp, with a large, painful egg on my forehead, I decided I was never going to change the Rabbit's oil filter ever again.

The local garage where they would do the tune-up was a nostalgic site. While no longer having bubbles on top of the gas pumps, it was replete with the old-fashioned in-ground service pits so that the cars did not have to be raised above the mechanic by a hydraulic lift. The two pits were each about twenty-four feet in length, six feet deep, and four feet wide with concrete stairs at one end. I hoped for their sake they had some sort of effective ventilation system installed for them, as well as in the garage in general, especially when motors were running. I didn't want some carbon-monoxide-addled mechanic working on my car.

Faust, curled around my neck, now seemed intrigued by the smells of grease, oil, exhaust and all the activity. He craned his neck to visually follow the number of people in grime-smeared dark blue coveralls rushing about, removing tires from rims, tinkering under vehicle hoods, and revving up engines.

Tapping him on the shoulder to get his attention, I asked him to promise that he would stay where he was and not try to touch anything. I had wanted to leave him home today as I had the car checked out but he mohwed and whined piteously, clawing the door to the garage for nearly thirty minutes. He shivered as if he feared I'd have a fatal accident when away from him which would leave him abandoned and alone—unable to find someone to scoop his litter box, open the steel cans of soft cat food, or give him his required full-body massages. He could be so melodramatic when he really wanted his way. Now he tilted his head in response to my request, still occupied by the activity around him, as if to say, "Yes, of course, Mom." He agreed like a two-year-old child. So I should have known better.

I was talking to John, the service manager, with whom I'd spoken on the phone when I made the appointment. He was heavy-set, close to fifty, with curly blond hair, and golden brown eyes set in a reddish face. His face was always tinted slightly magenta which made me wonder if he had inhaled too much car exhaust, drank excessively, or was constantly on the verge of apoplexy from hypertension. Still good looking, he must have been hot in his younger days. I could picture him tanned, slim, and flaunting his six-pack abs at Nantasket Beach, the Cape, or even at Farm Pond in Sherborn.

Faust was still rubbernecking but staying put. Everything was fine until a mechanic replacing a tire one bay over turned on a whirling pneumatic lug nut torque wrench. Faust panicked. Talons penetrated my shoulder muscles. I could feel his body become rigid. Instantly, he escaped from my shoulders. Hitting the stained concrete floor running, he disappeared, his blue leash fluttering behind him.

"Dammit," I bellowed through clamped teeth. "You promised." Fear dripping into my voice, I called out his name, commanding he return immediately. "Faust, You had better get yourself back here this very minute." As I surveyed the premises, there was no sign of any gray fur movement. He usually came when I called so I tried again. "Faust," I called louder now, "Come here."

I was trying to sound calm without a hint of anger but all the coverall-clad bodies stopped working to stare at me. Taking advantage of the moment, I called out to those assembled, "Hey, if any of you sees a gray cat with a blue harness wandering around, please let me know. He was frightened by the noise." I saw a few heads shake and heard a couple of chuckles and oks as they went back to work.

I told John I'd watch carefully for Faust as he pulled my 1975 Rabbit in over the nearest service pit. The car in place, one of the mechanics stepped down into the grime-covered pit and attached a work light to the undercarriage to inspect the steering system, suspension system, and drive train. He called out to John to check the car's mileage. "Nearly 40,000" came reply.

Then he called out to me, "The manufacturer's recommendations for a 1975 VW is to grease the front axle every 15,000. So, if it's okay with you, I'll go ahead and do that as well as check for wear of other moving parts." He was also going to change the oil, check the air-conditioner refrigerant and spark plugs, then rotate the tires. I admit I hadn't been taking the now nine-year-old car into be serviced with any regularity as it grew older and older. But, I absolved myself. I hadn't put that many miles on it each year and I dutifully took care of the basics myself.

Since I hadn't memorized every word of my car's owner's manual, it all sounded reasonable to me. Besides, I'd known John from when I first moved to Sudbury. Generally it was he who took care of my car himself, and he never charged me very much. More often than not, if he found something minor that needed work, he'd just tweak it for free.

Whenever I showed up at the garage, his face would glow with a big smile. While he was generally very coordinated, sometimes as we engaged in conversation walking to his office, he would almost trip over himself. I think he liked me but fortunately never made a move on me, always acting like a gentleman and friend. If he had acted otherwise, it would have been very uncomfortable. I knew his wife had been ill for years. Some men in that circumstance might have pursued extra-marital relationships, but either John didn't or he did it elsewhere. I was just grateful he never approached me in that vein. He was too good a mechanic to lose over sexual rejection.

Surreptitiously, I moved around the garage, calling Faust's name. The mechanics ignored me.

Then something slim, gray, and vertical moved behind a silver Pontiac. "Faust," I called. He peeked around the left front tire, lifted his whiskers to match his tail position, looked extremely pleased with himself, and casually sauntered toward me. Just then a car horn blasted. Fur on end, he ran again as if pursued by a cheetah and slipped unknowingly under a Chevrolet which covered the dark depths of the other service pit.

"Over here!" came a strangled voice. A tall mechanic who was quickly climbing out of that service pit was pointing under the car. "He's in here."

I raced over, picturing Faust in my mind lying on the pit floor with a broken back. I knelt down to barely glimpse a terrified Faust hanging precariously from the work light suspended from the Chevy's undercarriage. Poor thing. He had slid under the car only to find there was no floor there. He now clung desperately to what was keeping him from falling. On my feet, I hurried to the pit's stairs, after the mechanic, taking the steps two at a time. I got there just as the mechanic was approaching Faust in hopes of removing his dangling body.

As he put his hands out, I shouted, "No, don't touch him. I'll do that. He's frightened and may bite you." I'd never known him to bite anyone but I needed to be the one to disengage him just in case.

"Let me at least unhook the light so you can reach him," he said, unintentionally reminding me of my short stature. It was galling. My mother was nearly 5'7" and statuesque. My father was 5'11". And my brother was 6'4". So how did I manage to be barely 5'3"? Consequently, my father unflatteringly referred to me as "pygmy"—something I did not appreciate.

Slowly the mechanic approached Faust. Since the light which had been on before Faust had bound himself to it, it was getting hotter, and no doubt heating the metal cage surrounding the light bulb if it wasn't aluminum. I hoped the mechanics' closer proximity and movements wouldn't add to Faust's anxiety. Cautiously, he reached inches above the petrified cat to remove the lamp hook from its moorings, switched it off, and lowered it to my level. We were pitched into near-total darkness.

Faust seemed frozen in place. As the mechanic held the lamp up in front of me, I began talking calmly to Faust. Slowly my eyes were adjusting to the low-light level. Leaning Faust's haunches onto my left shoulder to give him some sense of solidity under foot, I worked to surgically detach his front paws, claw by claw, from the light cage.

Once one paw was free, he quickly released the lamp with the other and substituted my upper body for his clinging. "Okay," I almost shouted in relief. At that the mechanic switched on the light and hung it again. I thanked him profusely and he gave Faust a tentative pat on the back.

As I ascended the pit stairs, Faust hugged me, his back legs folded against my chest and his front paws around my neck. Nuzzling his face into my neck, he began giving me licking kisses on the chin as if to say, "I'm sorry, Mom. Can't we be friends again?" I rolled my eyes. "Okay. I'm glad you're okay. But..."

I stopped. There was nothing further to say. There was no way to scold Faust for disobeying me. I'm sure he didn't see his behavior that way anyhow. While his big adventure hadn't turned out quite as he had expected, filled with panic instead of fun, it definitely had been an "adventure." Maybe he had learned something from it all. As I looked into his glimmering amber eyes, I thought, "Yeah, sure. *I* was the one who had learned something: *Too soon old and too late smart.*"

Within ten minutes of my having descended into the grungy pit, Faust and I were finally out in the daylight again, with him once again hunkered around my shoulders. This time I had his grease-spotted leash which was still attached to his harness firmly wrapped around my right hand. Out the corner of my right eye, I could see his front paw pads looked red but, thankfully, were unburned.

While Faust and I were playing catch outside with a pink rubber eraser I had borrowed from the office, the Rabbit's tune-up had been finished. Feeling a little sheepish, I found John to pay my bill. As I tried to look appropriately penitent—I had to admit to myself that today had pretty much been business as usual with my evil-twin feline—I promised John I would never bring Faust to the garage if the car needed work again. Well, that was, of course, unless he could stay in the car. John smiled and shook his head knowingly. "Yeah," I responded, "best laid plans of mice, men, and cats ..." He laughed, rubbed Faust's head as if for luck, and disappeared back into the garage.

5

FIRST, DO NO HARM

The trip to the Desert of Maine was to be the next day. Faust and I packed light for an overnight trip, taking his carrier, several cups of litter and portable litter pan, some dry cat chow, a small bag of cat treats, two steel cans of soft food and a can opener, his dishes, and his special knapsack in which he rode when he tired of walking or curling around my shoulders. In addition to an emergency change of clothes, I packed my toothbrush and toothpaste, hiking boots, floppy sun hat, four granola bars, four Golden Delicious apples, two liters of water, and a deck of cards. I was teaching Faust three-card Monte.

In all the chaos I hadn't checked my answering machine. The red light was blinking. There was a message from Faust's new veterinarian, Dr. Bridges. She stated that there was a problem with Faust's recent blood work results. Last week he had been to the vet for his annual physical. Because of his early survival challenges he had pulmonary fibrosis which acted like asthma if he exerted himself too much. At that time there was little one could do to help him if he had difficulty breathing except to get him to calm down as quickly as possible. But other than that he was generally healthy.

She said his blood chemistries report showed his glucose level was 289 mg/dL where normal range for cats was 65-135 mg/dL, strongly suggesting diabetes. His urine likewise showed higher sugar as well as bacteria, increased ketone bodies (by-products of fat metabolism), increased lipase and amylase enzymes indicating pancreatic inflammation, and a negative change in serum electrolytes.

My mouth dropped open. I was stunned. She wanted to see Faust immediately. I called her back and we drove to her office, exceeding the speed limit all the way. Surprise of surprises, there were no police around. One time when I was leaving the house, I managed to exceed the 30 mph limit by two miles and, by golly, there was a cop waiting to give me a ticket.

The diagnosis of diabetes surprised and confused me. Faust didn't seem unduly thirsty or drink a lot. He didn't urinate frequently or vomit. His appetite was healthy and enthusiastic but not ravenous. He was never excessively hungry. His weight hadn't changed. Moreover, he was active and not lethargic or seemingly depressed.

Dr. Bridges showed me the chemistry results but they didn't make any sense to me. I was not convinced and explained my skepticism. "I just can't believe he has diabetes given his lack of symptoms," which I ticked off on my fingers. "Rather than act on those blood and urine analyses,

I prefer you repeat them both first." I didn't want Faust to receive an insulin injection or other medication to address his alleged health concerns when there was a question about them.

Dr. Bridges, said, "I hear your concern but his reported glucose level could be lethal. Still, he looks bright and perky. And, as you say, he's shown you no physical illness-indicative behaviors to support what the chemistry levels demonstrate. But if he's diabetic, I'd hate to wait another seven days to treat him. If we could somehow speed the process along, perhaps a day or two hopefully wouldn't make a significant difference. I certainly don't want to treat him for it if he's not diabetic." She agreed to re-test.

So poor Faust had another spot on his neck shaved of his handsome gray fur for the blood to be drawn. Fortunately his bladder was able to provide another sample of urine as well. Rather than automatically send the specimens off to her regular lab, Dr. Bridges went into her office to do some checking on alternatives.

She returned to the examination room looking relieved. She said, "I've found another laboratory that says it can analyze the samples and get me the results in less time. I can further speed the process by having one of my technicians drop off the specimens at this lab immediately. If they get them today, they can have the results for us in one but more likely two days max. That would be excellent. I'll call you the moment I receive their fax. In the meantime, keep an eye on him."

Faust and I left. I felt somewhat relieved. But the moment we arrived home, I found myself monitoring his every behavior. While I didn't believe he was ill, I worried that perhaps I had somehow simply missed possible diabetes symptoms or misinterpreted them. I knew I would never have ignored anything even slightly out of the ordinary ... and I was well aware of what to be aware of in humans with diabetes. My mother had married a man who struggled with it.

Poor Faust. As I closely followed his actions, riveting my gaze on them but pretending I wasn't, he sensed my concentration on him. No matter what he was doing, he would stop to look at me. It was as if he were trying to tell me that he didn't understand what's going on: "You're making me feel uneasy, Mom, maybe even guilty but I don't know for what."

While he hadn't done anything wrong, now his whole body seemed to droop. He wasn't a suspect of some criminal act so why was I treating him like that? His normal joie de vivre seemed to drain out of him, making him look as if he weren't feeling well. Suddenly he was no longer acting like himself, no longer acting as he had just before we went to the vet.

Like humans, cats don't like being stared at. It makes them uncomfortable, irritated, and aggressive. His being the center of attention of a worshipful crowd was one thing. But what I was doing was "surveillance" ... and an intimidating invasion of his privacy. Now he appeared self-conscious about anything and everything he was doing and he did not like it. Furthermore, he indicated, he didn't like me for doing it.

It was beginning to put a strain on our relationship. When I'd call him to sit beside me on the sofa, he seemed to have to stop to think about it first. Then maybe he would and maybe he wouldn't. This had never happened before. I used to call him and he'd race to wherever I was. I'd tell him that the *Rockford Files* was coming on and he'd locate the remote controller, clamp his jaw around it, and drag it across the rug to me. If I gave him the opportunity, he'd even push the large power button on it. Then he'd curl up with me to watch Rockford's fun and exciting exploits.

At present he seemed to check me out and stay where he was in case I was angry with him. I was baffling him and making him anxious and fearful. There was no way I could expect him to be able to see that all I wanted to do was detect a problem if one existed. Instead, my actions were precipitating his abnormal behavior. As a consequence, if I kept up this behavior, there was no way I could make an accurate determination of any diabetes symptoms. I shook my head at myself.

With that aha! I eased off my close and constant observation. I pretended to ignore him for a while. And that made all the difference. Cats are very smart and aware of their environment. Consequently, two hours later when I tossed the

Wiffle Ball to him, he sprang at it. With verve he swatted it around then stood up, and, with one paw, hurled it back to me.

This, I thought, was not a sick cat. But just to make sure, I took the four-foot-long knotted piece of cotton clothesline and trotted around from room to room dragging it behind me. He was right there, trying to grab and bite it. He was fast and having a great time showing off his much-esteemed athleticism, if only for a short time because of his incipient wheezing.

I picked him up and sat on the sofa with him in my lap. "Faust," I said with overflowing enthusiasm, "We're still going on our trip but it will be just a few days later." He looked at me with eyes wide, pupils enlarged. "We'll drive to Maine early one morning. You can act as navigator. We'll look at sand dunes, get you some ice cream, and then we'll stay overnight where you can check to see if they have any mice. And the next day we'll take some rides and play on the beach at the water's edge before heading back. You'll love it."

For one and one-half days I was fidgety, still worried that perhaps even though Faust didn't act it, he was ill. If he really had diabetes, would he go blind even if we put him on insulin right away? Would he have circulation problems and develop gangrene in his limbs? What about infections, abscesses, and organ failure? What about his so-called "pancreatic inflammation"? As I tried not to think about all the possible implications of these being his true blood-sugar and urine readings, I re-packed our trip gear several times.

Like a person possessed, I dusted and vacuumed the house until there was no nap on the living room rug. Furthermore, the top of the refrigerator, which had long been ignored, plainly became a "high priority" and now gleamed. I was running out of mind-numbing mechanical tasks to undertake so I sanitized the counters with bleach. I dried them carefully so Faust wouldn't get any of this cat poison on his paws or tongue.

To my surprise, however, at the first sharp whiff of the bleach, Faust trotted into the kitchen. Apparently the molecules had reached him quickly in the living room and like a siren's song beckoned him. With no hesitation he jumped onto the counter near the stove. Frenetically he sniffed, rolled, and sensuously rubbed his cheeks and back, from shoulders to tail, on the Formica, like a female cat in heat. He was purring ecstatically, bicycling with his feet. This amazed me. I would have assumed that since cats have a highly-developed sense of smell, he would have been repulsed by the smell of bleach. Obviously, I couldn't have been more wrong. There was something about it that had the same wild effect as catnip. His was practically orgasmic activity.

After marveling at him for a few minutes, I picked him up to put him on the floor. It was then he sniffed my hands. I hadn't used gloves when I cleaned the counter though I had washed my hands carefully afterward. Suddenly my hands were the recipient of his rapturous rubbing attention as well. At least that was a whole lot more acceptable than a small dog attempting to hump my leg. Ew!

When the phone finally rang late that afternoon, I grabbed it. It was a distressed-sounding Dr. Bridges. Oh, No! My panic-shuddering heart plunged into my legs. It was going to be bad after all, in spite of Faust's apparently glowing health.

"I don't understand it," she began. "His glucose level and urine are fine, within normal limits. How can that be? Stress could have made his blood sugar rise temporarily but the signs of pancreatic inflammation and bacteria in the urine? Not remotely possible. I'm nonplussed. I don't know how to account for this large discrepancy."

I let out a huge exhalation. Faust was fine after all—as if his bleach-related behavior hadn't spelled that out on a Broadway marquee. As if sensing things were better, he walked over to me where I was perched on the arm of the sofa and wrapped his tail around my leg. I leaned over to give his back a long pet. My mind was swirling around the chemistries' discrepancy.

"Maybe it was a lab error. I'm not suggesting they didn't analyze Faust's samples correctly, but, maybe they sent another cat's report to you with Faust's label. If that's the case, some poor cat isn't getting its proper medical treatment."

"I'll check with our regular lab immediately to let them know about the apparently mislabeled results. I'm so glad Faust missed that bullet. By the way, how is he doing today?"

"He's his perky self, thank goodness. Let me know what you find out. I'll delay our trip a few more days until this is resolved, just to make sure."

The next afternoon Dr. Bridges called again. "Well, I don't know how they figured it out, but you were right. They had somehow managed to mislabel the blood chemistry reports. I have Faust's correct report which is fine, just as his second report showed. And the vet of this ill cat has received his corrected report. That kitty's owner will be receiving some bad news but, at least, that cat will be started on appropriate treatment soon ... I hope soon enough. I also hope that sort of thing doesn't happen often. I've never encountered it before, at least not that I know of."

Delighted beyond words, all I could do was grin. "Thanks for the heads up ... from both of us. We'll be on our way to Maine tomorrow." Faust was curled up on the sofa as I hung up. "Guess what! We're off tomorrow morning on our next trip. Are you as ready as I am?" Faust raised his head slightly, lifted his whiskers, twitched the tip of his tail, and buried his head in my lap. Yeah, he was ready.

6

"ROAD TO MOROCCO"

The plan was to start early in the morning to go directly to the desert. We would then take our time looking around. I'd made reservations to stay overnight at the Windsor Cabins at Old Orchard Beach where we'd check out the beach and Palace Playland, an amusement park, then head home before commuter traffic became heavy.

My itinerary had us taking Rt. 27 northwest from Sudbury, passing through Maynard and Acton in order to pick up I-495 in Littleton. From there we'd head north through Lowell and Lawrence. In Amesbury we'd take I-95 to I-295 at Portland, Maine, and on to Freeport. In Freeport we'd turn left at Exit 20, we'd drive two miles on Desert Road to the desert where the road ended. Before us would be the vast Desert of Maine. It would be a piece of cake. The trip was only 140 miles which would take us approximately two and one-half hours depending upon traffic. Starting early would give us lots of time to explore the long, thin desert which ran north and south.

As we drove the next morning, the day was sunny with Baroque blue skies and only wispy clouds scudding across it. I hadn't see Faust this excited in some time. Anticipating a new exciting experience, he stood on the passenger seat, instead of lying on my lap or around my shoulders. His front legs were braced against the dashboard. He watched through the windshield, head on a swivel. Every so often he would seem to hop from one back leg to another, like a toddler needing a pit stop, as he strained to see everything that we rapidly passed. I was surprised how long he kept this up. He was in fine form, and, best of all, healthy.

Once we had arrived at the Desert of Maine, I changed into my hiking boots and positioned the still-excited Faust in his knapsack which I hung on my back and protected him from the sun with my large-brimmed floppy hat. As I approached the admission desk, Faust poked his front paws out and looked at the person seated there ... only to receive the hairy eyeball from the young ticket taker with bright red lips, kohled eyes, stringy hair, and heavy chains round her neck, reminiscent of Madonna in *Desperately Seeking Susan*.

"Hey," she said high-handedly, "there are NO animals allowed in here." She looked as if she were about to wag her authoritarian finger at us. "We don't want any animals crapping in the sand, tearing up the vegetation, or scaring any of our 'indigenous wildlife.'"

I was taken aback. I hadn't seen any prohibitions on pets in any articles I'd read about the Desert. But mostly I was particularly irritated by her overbearing manner. Faust made a dismissive snorting sound from his knapsack.

"Hold on a second. Hold on!" came the three-pack-a-day voice of a rough-hewn, angularly bony, gray-haired, man in his sixties who was rushing over to us from the 200-year-old building behind her, which looked as if it were the last remaining evidence of the old Tuttle farm. Trying to maintain a smile and not sound patronizing, he calmly said, "Brenda, That's not accurate. Actually we welcome pets here at the Desert of Maine. I'm sorry for the confusion."

Nodding toward the young woman who pursed her lips, pressing her teeth together, he continued, "Brenda's new here. She just joined us a week ago ..." he paused, "and we're delighted to have her with us. As for pets, they're welcome. All we ask is that you keep your pet on a leash and clean up after your animal. You know, scoop and bag. We have refuse containers all around for the filled bags. I can provide you with a kitty bag if you need one." I took one from his extended hand. "Oh, by the way," he added, "here's a brochure I think you'll find informative. I hope you and your cat enjoy your visit. If you have any questions, we're right here." I could see good ol' Brenda baby really champing the bit to be helpful.

"Thanks," I said and Faust gave him a soft mohw. He smiled but Brenda merely looked to the heavens and emitted a soft harumph. The set of her jaw remained. I wondered how long she was going to hang around after being corrected, even though he had done it nicely. I could hear her thinking, "Buzz off, Pops! This isn't Disneyland. I don't need this crap for the paltry sum you're paying me. As soon as I can, I'm outta here."

We started hiking the super-fine sand. Nearly the moment we stepped onto it, everything felt hotter. Moreover, the glare off the sand was stronger than I had experienced from sand in general. Checking the brochure, I saw that it addressed both those sensations. Apparently the sand was silt from mica deposits which reflected both heat and light. I hadn't expected such a startling change and was glad to have had my sunglasses and hiking boots. Too bad Faust didn't have his own versions of them. At least he had sun protection while ensconced in his knapsack.

As we walked to the north, we could see forests of fir trees creating a natural fence. In fact, trees bordered the desert from north to south and on the east and west. Occasionally isolated clumps of wildflowers sprung up out of the sand. According to the brochure, this was "'Perky Sue,' a drought-resistant and drought-tolerant evergreen native plant that thrives in low-fertility, well-drained soils in Zones 4 through 10." They looked well-adapted to this harsh environment with their short, sword-like green leaves, ten-inch slim stems which were topped with a single "sprightly yellow-petal flower with an orange center that attracts butterflies." Contributing to its survival here was the fact that it was resistant to both rabbits and deer, but, I suspected, maybe not to cats.

I removed Faust from his knapsack, checked the swivel hook and plunger latch attachment of his leash to his harness, and let him explore the flower. He sniffed and rubbed his face against it. I asked, "Do you want to walk for a while?" Silly question. Of course, he did, in spite of the warmth of the sand underfoot. He pulled on the lead and started toward something sticking out of the sand some twenty feet away.

Struggling to gain purchase was a young pine tree, only about eight inches tall, that was sprouting from what looked like a dead log ninety-percent buried in the silt. This intrigued Faust who after rubbing his whole body against the still-too-flexible tree-to-be seemed to be considering if he wanted to taste it. It took only one needle to convince him this plant was barf-worthy and he spit it out. The resinous taste was sure to linger as a reminder of his impulsive taste-testing.

The brochure indicated that there were wild blueberries and mushrooms present but I didn't spot any. If Faust had, he would have checked them out. I did see a hawk land in one of the conifers but disappeared amongst the smaller branches, perhaps to wait for a mouse or rabbit to scurry by. I picked up Faust just in case. Who knew if that hawk were currently hungry enough to attack a cat ... this cat. I knew what owls could do and wasn't going to wait to find out about this hawk.

The wind suddenly picked up. A powerful gust

swirled the sand around us. I buried Faust's muzzle in my chest. But in doing so, I caught the sandblast full in the face. I tried to cover my eyes, nose, and mouth but the damage had already been done. At least my eyes had been protected by my sunglasses which now sparkled with starburst patterns as the sunlight danced around the newly-pitted lenses. My nose needed blowing to remove the sand grains. Spitting and drinking from the plastic bottle of water I had attached to my belt eliminated most of the tooth-grinding particulate matter. Faust demurred when I offered water in my cupped hand. He wanted to get down again and continue his expedition for hidden treasures.

The brochure stated the desert had had a real, honest-to-goodness camel or two at one time to add to the ambiance. In this windy, sand-blasting environment, similar to the deserts of Africa, camels could manage better than most other animals. Their long eyelashes protected their eyes from the stinging, blinding, wind-blown sand and their nostrils partially closed to keep out the grit. However, it turned out the owners hadn't fully researched the camel and its infamous behavior. As a result, they had had to reconsider having these iconic desert dwellers after several "thorny incidents."

Not being the most social of animals, and easily agitated, camels, like others of their species, spit to warn off "predators"—wolves primarily, but also people. But we're not talking just a little saliva. No, camels need to be able to project this spit ... and saliva alone, which is very light by itself, doesn't travel the required distance with the required punch. So somehow camels had developed a way to regurgitate stomach juices to mix with their saliva. The result is a nose-hair-curdling, vomit-precipitating mass which would project further to issue a real attention-getting warning.

Apparently, if the tourist attraction owners knew this, somehow this essential and strategic piece of information didn't get disseminated at all or quickly enough to the desert visitors. When the camel's cheeks began to bulge, they were filling with their vile spit. This meant "duck and cover" ... or else. As a consequence, numbers of visitors unceremoniously received an unexpected, gag-producing wet glob, smack in the face or decorating their clothing. As one might expect, the camels soon departed the scene. Even in a slightly less litigious time than today, I wondered what the liability was for camel spit. Would stomach-twisting disgust have any monetary value?

After several hours of sun-scorching desert hiking, much of which Faust did in his knapsack or around my neck since he paws were risking sand burns, we rested at a picnic table under a copse of pine trees. We had a bite to eat and lots to drink. Neither of us was very hungry, mostly parched. I had an apple and Faust had a teaspoon of Friskies canned chicken paté. While I chugalugged from the plastic water bottle, Faust slurped from his water dish I had retrieved from the car. Refreshed despite our sweaty, silicate-varnished bodies, we headed back to Freeport proper to check out the famous L.L. Bean outlet store at 15 Casco Street.

For years I had received L.L. Bean catalogues which offered all kinds of outdoor clothing and recreation equipment. My being on their mailing list was likely the result of having purchased, years before, a holly berry-decorated balsam Christmas wreath for the inside of my front door. It emitted the most deliciously festive scent for months. The catalogue's layout was always woodsy and nostalgic for a less urbanized time in America. Emphasizing the rustic, the photos were of fireplaces with logs burning, colorful cotton or wool braided rugs, Arts and Crafts-styled furniture in pine, and yellow Labrador retriever puppies lying blissfully on large, dark green or plaid dog beds.

When Faust and I arrived at 15 Casco, Bean's original and flagship outlet store, we parked in front of the two-story beige building with its vertical siding, unpainted porch with natural pine railings and balustrades, and its signature green roof. Freeport had become known as an outlet store haven, where manufacturers sold their stock directly to the public, cutting out intermediaries, with one retail store after another lining the street.

Established in 1917 as primarily a Maine boot factory, L.L. Bean had come a long way on its journey to become a global company which now offered all manner of outdoor clothing, backpacks, tents, firearms, and fishing poles. I'd read that helping Bean expand its fame was gonzo journalist

Hunter S. Thompson who mentioned L.L. Bean in his 1971 book, *Fear and Loathing in Las Vegas: A Savage Journey to the Heart of the American Dream.* Ostensibly about a Mexican-American journalist killed by the LAPD, overall it appeared to be more like a bemoaning of the failure of the 1960's counterculture movement, one that Thompson never seemed to leave behind in his own life.

In his book Thompson relates how he, in a drug-induced miasma, leaves the Fillmore Hotel in San Francisco on his British BSA 650-cc Lightning motorcycle and roars across the Bay Bridge at one hundred miles per hour, wearing only a sheepherder's coat and ... wait for it ... his *L.L. Bean shorts.* And that "glowing reference" became an international ringing endorsement for Bean.

For safety sake Faust was in his knapsack on my back as we wandered around this cornucopia of outdoor and indoor goodies. In the camping area there were bottles of iodine tablets and of chlorine to kill bacteria and hopefully kill giardia—parasitic protozoan which is the most common cause of waterborne disease when you can't boil the water taken from the stream or lake. There were first-aid kits, collapsible stainless steel drinking cups, small pot-metal cylinders to keep camping matches dry, plastic packages of fire starters, bags of freeze-dried foods, tent pegs, and all kinds of compasses. It was like a candy store for outdoors people.

All the smells, colors, and textures combined to intrigue Faust too so he tried to crawl out of his conveyance to sniff, touch, knead, and play with whatever lay on tables or lurked folded in large, open wood cubbyholes. I couldn't have agreed more with him. There was something magical about the vastness of the array of merchandise and the enormity of all the clothing piled high in bins.

In a room off to the left were all kinds of coats, from rain gear to flannel-lined, quilted coat-shirts to down jackets and vests to pea coats. The pea coats grabbed my attention. After I had been graduated from Millis High School, my mother and I went to the Army-Navy Surplus Store in Framingham, MA, to see if they had any pea coats. These surplus stores helped distribute the over-abundance of government-issued supplies which had been accumulated during previous wars, providing amazing bargains for hunting and camping gear and casual clothing.

Interestingly, "pea coat" came from a Dutch word meaning a rough-textured, heavy fabric worn by fishermen. The dark blue/black coats of boiled wool were very heavy, substantial, and cold-resistant. I could see how they would be particularly useful for Navy personnel in keeping out wind, rain, sleet, snow, and ocean spray.

But since these were sized only for males at this time, they didn't fit around the smaller and differently-curved female form all that well. The density of the wool made my arm movement somewhat restrained. I admit I worried about frigid winds insinuating themselves wherever the fabric and my body didn't quite mesh. Still they were well-suited for Massachusetts winters. Moreover, the price for coats for my mother and me was very reasonable.

While Mother was paying for them, I drifted around the store, exploring to find kapok-filled life jackets. Before kapok, flotation devices used cork. And after kapok, they used foam. There were also WWII U.S. Army gas masks. One dark khaki-colored gas mask was listed as a "M3A1 Diaphragm Gas Mask and Military Respirator," available with its filter and carrier. As I was examining the straps to hold the mask onto the head and the flexible hose, I saw a note attached which indicated that a plastic "voice-mitter" and exhale valve component were used in place of the earlier metal version. I guess that was supposed to be progress. I was contemplating the horrors of chemical warfare when my mother tapped me on the shoulder. It was time to leave. This Army-Navy Surplus Store held so much history and memories of all kinds for everyone who had grown up in that particular era.

Even though the pea coat wore like iron, over time I became disappointed that it kept me comfy only as long as an arctic wind wasn't swirling around my upper legs or trying to seep in around the loose-fitting collar, which always required me to wear a wool scarf. Furthermore, the constricting fit of the sleeves became an annoyance. It meant that I had to be careful what I wore underneath the coat if I wanted to be able to move my arms in a hurry. This was of particular concern when I was driving because the coat made me feel as if I had both arms in plaster casts. Finally, I donated it like-new to the Salvation Army knowing someone whom it would fit better would be toasty.

Now for the fun of it I thought I might try one on again to see if the design had changed for retail. However, as I removed the knapsack, Faust made it clear he wasn't interested in sitting quietly in it on the floor while I did. That made it an inadvisable move. His curiosity was piquing. He wanted to move, run, explore, and discover. And there was so much more to discover. Besides, trying on the coat made no sense. Not only was I not going to buy one but also I was covered in layers of sweaty grit from the Desert.

After slipping Faust's knapsack back on, I walked out of the room to head for the staircase to the second floor, a short distance away. Faust was leaning back, looking up, stretching to see something. I craned my neck to look too. Above our heads was a large green canoe which hung from the ceiling by fine filaments that one couldn't see. Its seeming levitation gave me a start.

Where the staircase made a right angle with the first-floor wall stood an nine-foot, stuffed gold-colored brown bear with a dished face, gaping mouth with lip-curled snarl, baring its several long, sharp teeth, with its powerful forearms outstretched. Its five-digit paws with four-inch straight claws were ready to attack. Faust recoiled as we climbed the stairs, growling louder and louder. This was the first time I had ever heard him growl.

"Shush, Faust. Please don't make your presence known." I could feel him strain against the knapsack. "Don't you dare even think about jumping out," I whispered to him through compressed lips. Reaching back with my right hand, I tapped him on his bottom through the knapsack, "Relax!" I seethed.

Once on the second floor, I saw crossed canoe paddles decorating the natural pine and dark-green trimmed walls. "Look, Faust," I pointed and joked, "If I found you a life preserver, would you like to go out in a canoe?" It was hard to tell whether he considered that even a possibility, being one who was averse to getting his body wet. Whether taking it seriously or not, he didn't bother to respond.

As I was waxing upon the human joys of canoeing down the Charles River which I enjoyed, he had begun to check out the tables of merchandise as well as the other shoppers. Mostly he was looking, not trying to touch anything. I continued to extol the virtues of camping and water sports as we circumnavigated the second floor until I saw a black cotton turtleneck on a wooden table to my right. It was something I could use in the fall. Spread out, it looked like a good fit so I folded it again and stuffed it under my arm. I was so pleased that Faust was being on his best behavior and told him so.

However, as we descended the stairs, Faust

surprised me with an apparent change of mind. He was no longer growling, intimidated by the huge bruin. In an instant he had wriggled out of the knapsack to grab the bear by the back of the neck. His hind claws rapidly lacerated the bear's humped shoulders. "Dammit, Faust!" I shouted under my breath, panic-stricken, looking around for enraged security personnel. I dropped my handbag and the turtleneck to the stairs to try to detach Faust. But Faust had already moved on to ferociously chewing the bear's short, rounded ear. He was dislodging clumps of its golden fur. Using both hands, shifting from right to left, from front feet to back paws, I managed to remove the deranged cat.

Sweating, holding him by the scruff of the neck with my right hand until I could grab his leash out of the knapsack, I looked for the nearest restroom. He was still in the throes of what looked like a "kitty 'roid rage," wanting to take on and beast in the best of two falls out of three. Once inside the bathroom, I tried to restrain him on the counter by the sinks. Faust was still zoned out in his assault mode. If he didn't calm down quickly, he would have an asthma attack. He had already begun to wheeze.

"Relax!" I commanded like a Marine drill sergeant. That startled him. If he continued to wheeze and couldn't get enough oxygen, he would panic and breathe harder to get it. That would make a full-blown asthma attack more likely and potentially lethal. As I stroked him and whispered soothingly to him, he started to breathe again more slowly. Even though he was still whistling slightly, at least was taking in more oxygen. Eight minutes later, he allowed me to slip him into the knapsack again. Then after a few more moments, his agitation lessened and his body seemed to slump down. At that point, I retrieved my handbag and the turtleneck and hustled to the register.

Outside, I slipped off the knapsack. Sitting behind the wheel of my Rabbit, I removed Faust and placed him on my lap to spend a few removing the bear hair from his mouth and paws. I tried not to think about the bear's now-ratty-looking, spittle-coated ear. Considering that the fur looked old enough to have insects taking up residence in it, I checked Faust's entire body for any crawling "companions." We lucked out on that score, I think.

7

PLAYING AT THE PALACE

Conveniently for Faust, Ben & Jerry's was next door to L.L. Bean. Since I'd promised Faust some ice cream, he curled himself around my neck and we alighted to walk over to the small green-marble-roofed building. It had a cooling, four-columned beige porch with a four-foot roof overhang. The protected service windows beckoned us. Going inside with him was probably against the Maine health laws.

Faust especially loved vanilla ice cream. I used to as well. Ben & Jerry's was the best. I could picture them carefully slicing open the long flat vanilla bean pods lengthwise and scraping the aromatic vanilla caviar out. Every now and then when we were near an ice cream vendor, even if it wasn't Ben & Jerry's, I would get Faust a pink plastic sample spoonful. Because of the cold he usually let it melt a little on a paper napkin or, preferably, in a cut-down paper cup when one was available, before consuming it with gusto.

However, as we approached the right-most service window on foot, a garishly-painted 1967 VW bus, filled with raucous teenagers hanging out the windows, pulled fast into the parking lot. 1960s music blasted. The bus tipped slightly to the right as it took the turn, appearing directionally unstable, perhaps from having a swing-axle. The split-screen vehicle, which probably had had a red body and white top originally, was covered in fluorescent swirls and stars in front with flower petals surrounding the headlights.

But what really caught my eye was on the sides of the bus. Paintings portrayed the undulating bold patterns reminiscent of Wes Wilson's psychedelic concert posters. One poster in particular was the Grateful Dead's 1967 concert at the Fillmore in San Francisco. Someone had tried to duplicate the pink, black, and turquoise design along the entire length of the bus body, under the windows, and across the cargo door on the right side. I wondered where they had found this vintage vehicle. It was certain to have seen some wild times that these current occupants had only heard long-in-the-tooth stories about.

Faust cringed. Since cats have sensitive hearing, I suspected his overwhelmed reaction was primarily from the nearly one-hundred-decibel sound. It was jackhammering my ears as well. As his body tensed, his back-feet claws were transformed into lethal talons with which he once again stabbed my trapezius muscles to cement his position. Too bad I didn't own Kevlar shoulder pads. Even though I tried to keep his nails trimmed, I was going to have permanent puncture wounds in my shoulders. We were temporarily stalled under the porch overhang as the noise dampened and the crowd disembarked.

Softly I spoke to Faust as I stroked his head, "It's okay, Faust. Just relax. The music is off. Even though the people are still boisterous, you can ignore them. They won't bother us." I encouraged, "Besides, you have to have your yummy ice cream. It's your favorite. It's Ben & Jerry's." Faust was staring at the bus people who were animatedly talking and laughing. "Come on, Faust. There's nothing to worry about. Let's get you your treat."

Before I became a vegetarian, I used to occasionally delight in Ben & Jerry's rich, mouth-wateringly, flavorful, velvety cold delicacies. And now as I recalled the lustful pleasure of savoring their ice cream, I could taste it once again: All that sugar, cream, and fabulous flavors, like the real vanilla. It never ceased to amaze me how sometimes re-experiencing that taste required merely smelling something similar. But at other times, it was simply the recollection of the circumstances in which I'd eaten the Ben & Jerry's that brought back all its lip-smacking hedonism. These days I enjoyed it vicariously through Faust.

However, as much as Faust rapturously loved his Ben & Jerry's ice cream, covering his face in its milky stickiness, attempting to devour every last molecule with his long pink tongue, he was totally disinterested now. I stood there, stroking him, waiting to see what the bus occupants would do. Would they go to the left-most service windows or to the door on the right side? If they went inside, ignoring him as they passed, maybe Faust would give in to his passion after all. But they didn't ... and neither did he. As they gathered around the left-most window, still talking loudly, laughing, and ordering, Faust and I casually slipped off the porch on the right side and eased on back toward the Rabbit. Fortunately they hadn't noticed Faust. I didn't know for sure how he would have reacted if they had, but I suspected he might not have thought of them as his devout audience.

The sky was quickly darkening, accompanied by a distinctive, heavy rumble. I made a suggestion to Faust, "Let's head down to Old Orchard Beach now. There's not going to be much for us to see here in the rain." Back in the safety of the car, Faust began to unclench, slowly extracting his claws from my bloody, pierced shoulders. I took that as a yes. Single droplets began raising small puffs of dirt beside the car.

By the time we reached Old Orchard Beach, the sprinkles of rain had devolved into a deluge of pint-size teardrops. My windshield wipers toiled hard but were poor competition with Nature's inclement whim. As a result, we drove more slowly and cautiously, often nearly blinded by the slashing sheets. When we finally reached 14 Ocean Park Road, we found our billeting for the night. Windsor Cabins consisted of six small, white, red-trimmed, green-roofed buildings which sat facing one another, forming an oval. Cabin doors were red and the windows had white shutters, each one decorated with two vertical diamond shapes. The cabins were snugly surrounded on two sides by tall, heavily-leafed shade trees.

Once Faust was secured in his carrier, I dashed through the drops to situate him inside our little home for the night before I started sloshing back and forth to lug in all our gear. Even though there wasn't that much to haul, I took in smaller loads each time to prevent it all from getting wet. In the meantime a puddle was forming in the depression in front of the cottage door. Wading in my hiking shoes, my clothing sticking to my body, and my glasses fogged into murkiness, I stumbled on the door threshold. I fell into the door jamb, barking my shins. My hair was streaming with rivulets still running down my face.

After I finished hauling, I stripped, dried myself off with the small bath towel, and changed clothing. Life immediately looked a little better. Faust had the rest of his canned chicken while I chowed down another Golden Delicious apple and granola bar. As much as I liked apples and granola bars, this two-day diet was quickly becoming monotonous. We re-hydrated ourselves and Faust used his temporary litter pan while I read a brochure located in the cabin on the four-acre Palace Playland we were to visit the next morning.

This was New England's only beach-front amusement park, operated since 1902, and our anticipated destination. I was excited. I couldn't wait. I was looking forward to riding their carousel which was renowned for its forty-four horses and two chariots. I'd always loved carousel horses, but especially those that were carefully, aesthetically renovated to recreate their original artistic glory, which this carousel promoted. It also had horses with all four feet off the ground, manes flying wildly, eyes wide, and nostril flaring. Making it even better was the carousel band organ which could make all kinds of orchestral and calliope sounds from a paper roll, like a player piano. We made bedtime around 9 p.m. in order to have an early start, but not before Faust and I played a few games of three-card Monte.

When Faust saw the deck of cards, he stood up on his chair at the small pine kitchen table. I sat opposite him and removed the Jack of Spades, Jack of Clubs, and Queen of Hearts from the deck, laying them out face up in front of him. Then I placed four pennies on the table in front of him as well. This was his betting money.

"Okay, Faust," I said picking up the Queen of Hearts, "This is the card you're looking for. I'm going to rearrange the three cards. Then you're going to bet and pick your card." I tapped the card with a finger. "Are you ready?" He looked up at me which I took as assent. "Okay, place your bet."

He waited a second so I tapped a finger near his pennies. With his right front paw he pushed a penny an inch toward me. I moved the three cards, now face down, around on the table then lined them up in a row. "Okay, Faust, Where's your card ... where's the Queen?"

He seemed to pause a second then slapped the middle card with his right paw. When I turned it over, it was the Queen. I gave him a cat treat. We did it three more times. And three more times he managed to find the Queen. I have no idea how he did it ... if his concentration was that good. Since I purposely didn't keep track of where the Queen was, I didn't think my body language was giving him a clue.

In spite of whatever perceptual or memory skill Faust possessed, there was no way I was about to let him near a real game ... and certainly not for real money. On the street three-card Monte was a traditional "short con," a quick and easy confidence game to separate the mark, the victim, from his or her cash. Players were shills, the dealer's associates, who would be winning and losing money. The mark would see that he or she could easily follow the location of the Queen when others couldn't. Once the mark bet, dealer might allow him or her to win once or twice. After that, using a little sleight of hand or misdirection, the dealer would make the Queen "change position." But the mark would be hooked and have to keep trying. Still, I had to wonder if Faust could follow the disappearing Queen, however it was manipulated.

Finding no mouse scent trails to pursue, Faust curled up with me in one of the twin beds. Awaking around eight a.m., rested and eager to get going, we were once again greeted by the disagreeably wet dreariness. After Faust and I had our breakfast, of sorts, I slowly began schlepping our gear back to the car. The time dragged. As ten o'clock approached, the opening hour of the Palace Playland, we hurriedly hopped into the car. But the weather system had diabolically stalled over us.

Arriving at W. Grand, Palace Playland's location, we could see the 1,770-foot pier before us, stretching out across the deep beach to meet the ocean. It was now constructed of steel, having been replaced a few years earlier after weather damage. But that was not the first time it had had to be replaced in recent years. One of those famous Maine blizzards had destroyed it as well in1978. Seemingly this historic site was a magnet for Nature's wrath. At the end of the famous pier was Pier Casino Ballroom where back in the 1940s and 1950s musical luminaries like Frank Sinatra had performed.

Stygian clouds of mist were boiling and hissing above. With intermittent heavy gusts, the pouring rain gave no sign of letting up any time soon. We parked facing the turbulent, roiling, dark and forbidding ocean, watching small whitecaps form to march in rows on the incoming waves, sending forth foamy sea water increasingly higher on the beach. There was no one around. Not even a stalwart soul walking on the beach with or without a dog. No one was soggily riding the Ferris wheel behind us in the Palace Playland complex.

Despite the seductive call of the carousal music which I could hear through our mostly-closed windows, I wasn't going to splash across the street with Faust, getting us both soaked, to ride the merry-go-round. And I wasn't going to leave him in the car alone to fulfill my wish. This was *our* trip to enjoy *together*. So far this day wasn't going too well. As we waited another hour, we watched the ocean become more sullen and flags on tall poles snap in the wet, chilled winds. Faust curled up in my lap and began making little twitching movements as if he were dreaming of chasing a mouse ... or, perhaps, tearing a stuffed giant brown bear limb from limb.

When the hour was up, the sky was still slate, featureless, and menacing. As the twenty-mile-an-hour winds, with gusts even higher, and rain changed direction, I had to periodically close one window and open another on the other side of the car for air. Now the rain was slashing the car sideways, drumming on the car's body. At times it had fallen so heavily it was as if someone had unloosed the contents of a water tower on us.

Wiping the fog off the windows once again, I caught in my peripheral vision some brilliance in the sky. Looking like a branching neural dendrite, it cleaved the upper atmosphere. It was followed quickly by a huge crash which seemed to rock the car. I didn't need to count the seconds between the flash and sonic eruption to know the lightning was close by. Too close for comfort. As a result, I capitulated to Nature.

We were not even going to walk on the beach, sift sand through our toes, look for shells, or examine the old pier's pilings. Faust was not going to have the chance to play with the froth as it thunderously rolled in, sucked bubbled pores in the sand, and then swooshed as it rolled back out. After he had had his first delightful experience on the beach in Rockport, Massachusetts, he was addicted. But, sadly, today was not going to be a recurrence.

At the crash Faust elevated off my lap and momentarily seemed uncertain what to do next. I tried to sooth him, "It's okay. It was just lightning ... but it's nearby. Too close. I think we should head back home. Is that all right with you?" He looked at me with still-wide eyes and mohwed pitifully. I gathered him back onto my lap, stroked his head, and started the car. When he tentatively squeezed himself into a tightly curled ball, I took that as a yes.

Ironically, as we left Maine, the weather began to clear. But from the size of the puddles that paralleled the road, it was evident it had been raining hard in New Hampshire too. I decided not to head toward the beach where the seashore sand would be soaking wet as well. One of these days Faust and I would take that long-discussed trip west to see the National Parks. Until then, we'd find some other, shorter excursions to enjoy together.

8

THE LADY VANISHES

Alix Brooke had been a dear friend—almost like a sister—ever since our childhood in Point Pleasant, New Jersey. She got her first name from the 1940s and 1950s actress, Alix Talton, whom her mother liked and thought her daughter resembled. She was tall and thin with lustrous, wavy chestnut-colored hair that she wore short, just below her ears. We were a mismatched couple. I, on the other hand, was shorter, heavier, with unremarkable shoulder-length medium blonde hair that I rubber-banded into a puny pony tail.

At that time we read Nancy Drew mysteries, adored my Tabby named "Peoples," and loved and shared really bad, groan-worthy puns. I thought at the time that puns were oh-so clever and terribly sophisticated. After all, if a pun was really called "paronomasia, a form of word play exploiting multiple meanings of a term or of similar-sounding words," I surmised it must be a "highly-intellectual exercise." We never lost our love for puns and fortunately over the years graduated to a better puns and a greater appreciation of them. They still elicited groans and giggles.

But our deepest shared interest was rooting for the Brooklyn Dodgers. In the 1950s eight-time All Star and great hitter, center fielder Duke Snider was my favorite player. Alix's was first-baseman, Gil Hodges. Alix and I watched as many games as we could together on her parents' Zenith Tyler black-and-white, twelve-inch porthole-screen console television. If only her family had had a color set because this was the first World Series televised in color on NBC.

We never dared to hope the Dodgers could pull off a win over the Yankees. But 1955 turned out to be a magical year for our Dodgers, as proclaimed loudly by the dulcet voice of radio and television announcer Vin Scully. After his famous introduction to each game, "It's time for Dodger baseball!" he would passionately describe the play by play. He was practically one of the Dodgers. What a joy to listen to throughout the seven anxiety-provoking games of the Series.

The lineup that year was without equal. We were elated. The players who stood out were Roy Campanella catching; Gil Hodges on first base: Jim Gilliam on second base; Jackie Robinson on third-base; Duke Snider at centerfield; Pee Wee Reese at short stop (a position I later played in high school softball when I wasn't substituting as catcher), Carl Furillo at right field, and Don Hoak at left field.

On that glorious day of the seventh game, which will always stand out in the history of my youth, there were several pitchers. Don Newcomb and Carl

Erskine pitched for several innings each but didn't continue. For some reason unknown to me, they both had sore arms, or so it was reported. That left it to southpaw Johnny Podres on the mound to finish off ... and, boy oh boy, did he ever ... BIG TIME!

There was no describing the thrill when "the Bums" truly trounced the Yankees four games to three. Alix and I jumped up and down, screamed, and whooped, knocking over a bowl of popcorn onto the throw rug under their maple coffee table. We had been stuffing in our faces as we agonized over whether the Yankees would get any runs and mess everything up. But on October 4, 1955, the guys in Brooklyn pulled it out with two runs to zero.

Hallelujah! This was IT! This was the Dodgers *first and only* time winning the World Series while still located in Brooklyn. *O frabjous day! Callooh callay.* "Beware the Brooklyn Jabberwock, we chortled in our joy." And, making it even sweeter, they had done it on the Yankees' home turf, Yankee Stadium! It was *too* fine!

My family and I moved from New Jersey to Massachusetts when I was fifteen but Alix and I remained in constant communication. In the beginning it was through letters but later it was phone calls which continued throughout the succeeding decades. Much later on, whenever I would drive to Jersey or she would drive Massachusetts, it was like a grand reunion of laughing, story-telling, and punning.

Twenty years had passed since we'd moved. Her parents had died a few years before in an automobile accident with a jack-knifed semi on icy I-495 on their way to visit her father's brother in Allentown, Pennsylvania. It was then she decided on a change of scene and moved to Massachusetts. Prior to leaving, she had worked for Bristol-Myers' pharmaceutical division as a researcher. In Massachusetts she had been hired by Biogen to work on a hepatitis vaccine. Settling in Wayland, west of Boston, she was about four miles to the southeast of my home in Sudbury.

Once she had moved, we got together once a week, generally on Wednesday. We'd always start at my house at noon and go from there. The reason for that was simple: Faust. Alix quickly became Faust's second-best friend. Well, I'd like to think I was "first," but, in truth, cats, even Faust, can appear at least temporarily fickle when it comes to other-humans' devotion and their skill at indescribably irresistible petting.

Faust always waited for her sitting on the back of chair by the front window, staring out with expectation. When she'd arrive, she always called out, "Plaaaaay ball." At the sound of her voice, Faust would run to the door in great anticipation and jump against it with his front paws like an excited Jack Russell terrier in slow motion. The moment she appeared in the open door, he'd leap into her arms, rubbing his gray face against hers, licking her partial right ear and her chin until her skin was bright pink, reminiscent of whisker burn.

The outer part of her right ear had been sheared off in an ice skating accident when we were fooling around on a frozen lake west of Point Pleasant in the town of Brick. Her skate blade had caught a root peeking above the ice, throwing her face down. Coming up behind her, I couldn't stop in time or completely swerve around her. I immediately dropped to the ice, thinking that would halt my movement ... so much for my understanding of the physics of the situation at that age. As it turned out my smooth coat's coefficient of friction wasn't that large so I kept moving toward her on my derrière, feet first.

I tried to use my hands and arms to re-position my body to get my sharp blades away from her. But my twisted movements were less than precise. Missing her body, my left skate slid imperceptibly close to her head. While I somehow avoided her scalp, I shaved a millimeter sliver off her external right ear. It all had happened in a matter of seconds though it had seemed like a half-hour. As soon as I could get to my feet, I grabbed a handful of snow from the shore both to preserve the tiny strip of removed tissue and slow the red flow from her ear.

My mother, who had been skating with us, had just gone back to remove her skates and sit in the car while she waited for us to finish. She saw everything that happened. Running onto the ice with her rubber-soled boots, she arrived at Alix's side one minute after I had excised her flesh. She picked her up and shuffled cautiously across the slippery terrain to get her into the car as quickly as possible. Off to the nearest Emergency Room, we nearly flew, well exceeding the posted speed limit. Incredibly, Alix, with snow still pressed to her ear, was seen within minutes. The waiting room had been all but empty. This was a miracle unto itself.

The doctors who saw her said the piece of tissue I'd rescued was too narrow to re-attach, but nice try. So they sutured and bandaged her ear, gave her a prescription for penicillin, and suggested she continue to wear her hair to cover that ear after it healed. Even though Alix dismissed my fervent need to continuously apologize, I never ceased to feel guilty about disfiguring her ear. That is, until she managed to get even with me a year later in a neighborhood softball game on the high school grounds.

Alix was at the plate. When she connected with the ball, she sent a steaming grounder toward me at short stop. I expected it to drop and bounce back up, letting me easily hook it with my waiting glove. That didn't happen. Instead of dropping, it sailed directly into my right kneecap, dislocating it in a fireworks burst of exquisite pain.

The x-rays at the ER showed the ball had not only dislocated my knee cap, damaged the articular cartilage behind it, stretched a patellar tendon ligament but also broke off bits of the patella which now floated freely around the knee joint. These bits were called "patellar mice." That was a cute name for an un-cute situation. That injury, which arthritis would later magnify, would haunt my running and other athletic efforts forever into the future. After that, I stopped apologizing.

When we'd get together on Wednesdays, the only day she'd take off from her six-day work week, we'd go out to lunch, the Boston Museum of Art, the Science Museum, plant nurseries, art galleries, folk festivals, walk the 1.7-mile shore trail around Walden Pond, and occasionally catch a movie, play, or concert. Faust joined us at many locations, casually draped around my neck, except at the museums, movies, plays, concerts, and restaurants, unless they were held outdoors. The one exception was Tanglewood, the summer home of the Boston Symphony in the Berkshire Hills, where he was not permitted, even on a blanket on the grounds at the concerts.

Surprisingly, even at some open-air locations and events where people were just milling around, there were a few who would comment theatrically that Faust's presence was "inappropriate." From our perspective, if we were abiding by the rules, acting civilly, and not intruding into or interfering with their activities, we didn't care what they thought or said. Besides, most people were amused and delighted to see Faust. They'd talk to him and maybe even pet him. And if they were very lucky, he'd return the favor with a dance step or two or some feline gymnastics. Those who had cameras with them snapped his performances. Kitty-grinning, he was always happy to oblige.

On those occasions when Faust had to be left

behind, he invariably demonstrated how offended he felt about being "abandoned" when we arrived back home. His primary tactic was to back up to my living room floor-length draperies and wiggle his tail and hindquarters as if firehose-blasting them with urine. In spite of this petulant display, I never saw any wetness or yellow staining so I never knew if he were only threatening to do it ... or did it ... and I just couldn't see it. If I had had a black light, it would have told the tale. He always cocked his head to one side after this display as if to say, "Well, I *could* have."

But I knew down deep he wouldn't have done that to me, no matter how disgruntled he was. He possessed integrity and a higher kitty moral character than that. This was simply a ritual to express how he'd missed being with us, enjoying our company ... and to blackmail us into taking him with us next time. Besides, as soon as we returned from our few and infrequent Faust-less trips, he always received a special goody, like some canned human salmon or pieces of solid white chunk tuna plus plenty of petting.

However, when the next Wednesday arrived, Alix didn't. She simply didn't show up, without a word. This was so unlike her. She would have let us know if something else had come up or if she were to be delayed. If her car had had a problem, she would have had someone call us for her, assuming she was able to. Punctuality was important to her because she felt it showed respect for the person waiting.

As we waited, we both were becoming increasingly concerned. At one o'clock I tried reaching her by phone but to no avail. At two, I did the same. By three, our concern crept over the boundaries into full-fledged panic. Faust still stood patiently on the back of the chair by the front window, his left paw placed on the glass, his tail waving above the fabric, eagerly anticipating her arrival. When he hadn't seen her or heard her voice as the time hobbled by, he looked confused and disappointed. His tail was now sharply slapping the chair.

I was sure something had happened to her. Perhaps she had fallen in her bathtub this morning. Or perhaps she had been in a car accident, either heading to or from work in Cambridge the day before. We had waited long enough before actually checking. With the extra-set of house keys she had given me in hand, Faust and I drove to her house to personally investigate.

There, we slipped inside. I loudly called to her as we threaded our way through the rooms of the one-story house. Her handbag wasn't there. There was no sign of a scuffle. Everything seemed as it should have been, except, of course, for her absence. Faust wandered around, sniffing everything of hers he encountered. In her bedroom his gravelly mowh started low in his throat then rose to a high-pitched screech. I picked him up to comfort him but he was too tense to respond. Next, we skulked around the property to see if she had fallen outside, while simultaneously checking the windows and doors we passed for signs of unlawful entry. But once again everything looked all right.

Her car, which she generally left outside, wasn't in the driveway. Consequently, I glanced through the garage side window. It was always possible she had decided to park it in there for convenience or because of automotive problems and taken a cab. But the car wasn't there. Even if it had been, I didn't know what that would have told me. Like Faust, I felt mystified and frustrated. My logical faculties were trudging hip-deep in emotional mud. Nothing made sense.

Before we left, Faust and I stopped by Alix's adjacent neighbors, Claudia Smissman on the right and Mara Flaherty on the left. Claudia had just run home from her office to pick up some contracts she needed. Mara who was a stay-at-home mom had just finished reading a chapter from *The Wizard of Oz* to her five-year-old daughter, Emily. They both said they hadn't seen Alix for the last two days. Moreover, neither one said she had heard or witnessed anything unusual. Claudia added that her snorting, ancient bulldog, "Winston," always reacted with barking to the sound of Alix's car next door. But Winston hadn't made a peep since Tuesday morning when Alix apparently left at her regular time. I gave each of them my business card. They promised to keep an eye out and call me if they saw her or heard anything.

Back home I phoned Biogen. It was only four o'clock so I expected to find everyone still there.

While administration tended to be 9-to-5 people, researchers weren't. With only a minimum of effort I reached her research assistant who told me that the last time the lab had seen her was on Tuesday morning. I was getting a stomach ache from all this.

I still needed to check out the hospitals west of Boston as well as in both Boston and Cambridge to see if she was listed as an inpatient. Discovering, locating, and calling them all—there were so many more than I had imagined—took fifty slogging minutes. Faust was lying like a ragdoll, listless on my lap as I went through the *Yellow Pages'* listings. No luck. But maybe that was good news? Maybe that meant she hadn't been in a car accident.

As far as I could tell, I was scraping the bottom of the barrel of possible actions I could take. I could call the Massachusetts State Police as well as the Boston and Cambridge Police to see if they knew anything. But I didn't have her plate number or the year and make of her car. But what the heck! With nothing to lose I tried them all the same. Still nothing. I had to admit that it finally looked as if I had run out of options. A sense of debilitating powerlessness enveloped me. I knew something was wrong. I also knew—hoped—that she would contact me when she could ... *if* she could.

Through the remaining week, I continued to call her home. Next Wednesday arrived and departed without a sign of Alix. Faust was downright depressed, slinking sluggishly around with a drooping tail. Perhaps he was feeling a little abandoned by Alix, not understanding how she, of all people, could do such a thing to him. I was beside myself, trying to think if there were something I was missing that I could do to try to locate her. Weeks rolled by but every Wednesday Faust religiously sat on the back of the chair by the window, scanning the street, hoping. Soon thirty days had passed.

As that next month moved along, Faust was barely touching his regular canned kitty food. His special human canned salmon likewise held little appeal. He even ignored his primo catnip. He was no longer dancing. Occasionally he went through the preliminary motions of playing with the knotted clothesline when I coaxed and cajoled, but his movements were spiritless and lasted only a minute. It was obvious his feline heart wasn't in it.

We still watched the *Rockford Files* together and he distractedly padded the television screen when NBC repeated a showing of Billy Wilder's 1944 film noir classic *Double Indemnity*. His only interest in the film was when blonde-wigged Barbara Stanwyk appeared. But even here his padding was listless. He didn't know why but Alix, his second-best favorite person in the world, wasn't around to give him her special brand of kitty love. He looked so bereft that I worried that he might possibly have wondered if he had done something wrong—to create a rift—to cause her disappearance. Guilt was a terrible emotion to have for humans or cats. In my darker moments I worried he might just fade away from grief.

9

POINT OF NO RETURN

On the forty-fifth day at one p.m., the phone rang. My heart stopped. I felt momentarily paralyzed, unable to respond. Was it going to be Alix? Or was it someone telling me she was dead. On the third ring I pushed my nerveless arm to pick up. As I answered, her oddly-distant voice echoed in my ear. Overwhelmed, my first reaction was a dizzying mixture of surprise, happiness, and anger. I wanted to scream at her, "Where the hell have you been? Dammit! We've been worried sick."

When the first words out of her mouth were, "I'm so sorry, I should have told you," her voice betrayed distress beyond mere guilt.

Something was very wrong. I swallowed hard and took a deep breath. I tried to picture myself relaxing on a tropical beach to calm myself and step back from my anger ... and my fear. She should have told me what? It had to be bad. I wanted to cry but Alix needed me. She had something important to share with me.

Struggling, I said, "Alix, It's so wonderful to finally hear from you. Faust and I have been *so* worried. Please tell me how you are ... and what's been going on."

"I'm not well." She paused, noticeably crying. I bit my lip, tears welling, dropping onto my tee-shirt. I wanted to be with her, to put my arms around her to comfort her. "Do you want the short version or the long?"

My heart skipped several beats and the room spun. "Take your time and tell me everything."

"As you may recall, I'd been having intestinal problems for many months. I didn't tell you the problem was getting worse because I didn't want to concern you … besides I had no reason to believe it was anything but Irritable Bowel Disorder. Well, that was what my doc had suggested it was. But then nothing seemed to help. Over time I gave up all kinds of foods to see if it would make a difference— you know, like an allergy or intolerance to them— but it didn't. I still was punished with lots of gas, bloating, pain, and diarrhea—all the really fun, glamorous stuff of life." She tried to chuckle. "Work was becoming impossible. I couldn't concentrate because the abdominal pain was increasing. Most of the time I just tried to ignore it as best I could and tried not to let it be too much of an inconvenience."

As she paused again, I tried not to be angry she had kept all this from me. But why couldn't she have shared it? Maybe I could have helped somehow. I began to recall that she seemed to use the bathroom more frequently and seemed to be taking a lot of Tylenol and Pepto-Bismol. I had asked her about it once but she had pointedly shrugged it off so I didn't ask again. I felt she would tell me when she was ready.

"You must have been in hellacious pain. You poor thing, that's awful!" I said. I felt on the edge. I breathed deeply, paused, and urged her to continue to explain.

When she spoke again after gulping a slug of liquid, her voice cracked, "I began having worsening diarrhea and frequently saw blood. My doc had already done x-rays of my gut using contrast mediums you swallow and also have pumped into your lower intestine. He followed those by an MRI." She stopped.

My heart was galloping in my chest. I now knew where she was going and I did not want her to go there. I was imagining her hazel eyes all puffy and red, her cheeks wet, dripping on to her favorite hand-made Norwegian sweater. That was the one with a cream-colored background and a red, green, ochre, and black woven design with its decorative pewter buttons. That was her outdoors "power" sweater. It was the one she always wore for skiing, ice skating, and snowshoeing.

Our past winter sports adventures ran double-time past my eyes. Of course, after my softball knee disability, I could no longer keep up with her as successfully in our athletic pursuits as I once could, often tagging along slightly behind. But that didn't matter because we were doing things together and having fun. Faust sometimes joined us. Occasionally I pulled him along, standing up, on one of her downhill skis when we went cross-country skiing.

With trepidation, I reluctantly prompted her to go on, "Faust and I are listening." At that, Faust, who had been lying in a fetal position on the sofa, suddenly jumped onto my lap, threw his paws around my neck, and snuggled close to my face, perhaps trying to listen too. It was as if he knew I was talking with Alix which suddenly made everything close to all right again.

"Adenocarcinoma." That single word was an exploding projectile hurling itself forward, etching itself indelibly in stone, demolishing unrealistic hopes, making her destiny unassailable. "By then I was no longer having constant diarrhea. Instead I could hardly have a bowel movement at all. Since I had been given an opioid for the increasing pain, my first question was whether the constipation was from the opioid."

My anger shifted to her physician. How could he have let this thing go on as long as it had? He didn't sound like the sharpest tool in the shed. I wondered how carefully he had really been following her. Sadly, I suspected it was a matter of out of sight, out of mind. When she was present, the doc focused on what had been done and what could still be done. I guessed if I were being honest with myself, I had to admit that perhaps he had no reason to think of zebras instead of horses. But if only he had, it might have given her a little more time.

"Then my doc consulted with Boston oncologists

who concurred that I should go to Dana-Farber Cancer Institute. They set up an appointment. I drove there ASAP. That was amazing." She half-chuckled, half-cried. "How likely is that kind of efficiency ever to happen again in medicine? Reminds me of my ear. Anyway, they did surgery, resected a huge mass they found in my transverse colon, and biopsied the removed tissue and lymph nodes." She heaved a sigh and paused for several seconds.

Okay, I'd heard enough. Now I needed to know where she was and what we could do for her. I asked, "Where are you now?"

Breaking into crying again, she seemed to ignore the question. Perhaps she was unable to hear me. She stopped sobbing and slowly proceeded as if in a trance, sounding more like her professional researcher self, "The biopsy showed the cancer had metastasized. It's a very aggressive cancer. They started me on 5-FU—Fluorouracil—a DNA synthesis inhibitor. The problem with that one-dose chemo is that while it was thought to improve 'quality of life'—whatever that was supposed to mean—clinical evidence showed it did nothing to prolong survival."

I didn't want to hear any more about this. But she desperately needed to tell me. I hung in there, holding down a cry of anguish.

"So," she continued, "I volunteered to be a guinea pig for some other experimental drug they were testing which likewise had no positive effect. They finished the protocol with radiation. That meant I got to spend my days puking my guts out. But ... but," she sounded out of breath and about to collapse, "but the cancer didn't respond to anything ... and ... they had run out of options."

Anger was replacing sorrow in her voice. "What a bitch!" she nearly shouted. "Would you believe there aren't even *any* experimental drugs today being tested that have even a remote chance against this super-aggressive malignancy? What did I do to deserve this? Hell, I should have been working on cancer rather than on a stupid hep B vaccine." She laughed sardonically.

I was numb. It was as if I'd been sucker-punched in the solar plexus. I wanted to double over in tear-soaked agony or raise my fist to the heavens to shout expletive recriminations against a stupid, uncaring, and cruel God. If He, She, or It existed, how could a so-called "Supreme Being" malevolently afflict my dearest childhood friend who was such a good, compassionate person who was doing important and necessary medical research? Instead of physically responding, I just sat there on the sofa, phone in hand. Faust was hanging on to me, perhaps trying to not only support me but also comfort us both.

I swallowed hard the grief but it was lodged in my throat like a strangling piece of food. Earnestly I said, "Faust and I want you to stay here in Sudbury with us. We'll care for you. We can get you whatever you need or want and take you to the doctor."

I could hear I was babbling, my voice rising,

speaking as fast as I could so she wouldn't say no. My stress level was peaking along with my blood pressure. I now understood with crystal clarity the unknown I had been so anxious about.

"No. That's so sweet and generous but I'm already at Wellesley-Weston Hospice on Wellesley Street, near Regis College."

Hospice? Oh, my god! Things were already so much worse than I could have imagined.

"I want to see the *both* of you. Promise me you'll come very soon AND bring Faust. You must bring Faust. I really need to see him."

"Can we see you today?"

"Yes, today!" she emphasized. "I don't want to sound overly dramatic, but, seriously, gets your buns over here. ASAP!"

Still in shock, I failed to ask Alix about visiting hours. I located the hospice number, called, and checked their hours but made a point of not asking about pets visiting. Even though the pet therapy movement for hospice patients was spreading, if this particular hospice hadn't gotten with those therapeutic marching orders yet, I didn't want to alert them to a potential feline trespasser. I didn't give a rodent's butt if they had rules to the contrary ... or armed security guards ready to haul my non-compliant derrière out of there. Faust was going to see Alix ... period. End of story. We were on a mission.

Faust and I quickly got our gear together.

Primary was his favorite knapsack. I planned to smuggle him in. If he didn't move his legs or stick his head out, we'd probably run the gauntlet without difficulty.

The hospice was an L-shaped, one-level, red brick building with glass front double-doors and lots of picture windows. It was richly landscaped with boxwood hedges hugging the building's foundation, colorful annuals—coleus ranging from chartreuse to purple, yellow and orange marigolds, mixed dwarf phlox, and red, light blue, and purple salvia in mulched, oval-shaped mounds—and three forty-five-foot maple trees serenely shading the front.

With Faust snuggled down, I headed for the entrance. In the subdued-light of the hospice foyer, I approached the desk to inquire about Alix's room number. Faust remained very still. He seemed to know we were playing a form of hide-and-seek with a formidable opponent and if he were very good, he'd see Alix. He was motivated to comply.

As we walked down the long, vinyl asbestos floor-tiled hall to the left of the front desk, looking for number 26, I noticed that the beige walls were hung with original art, perhaps done by the residents or were donations. The oil or acrylic canvases were painted in bright colors—subjects were realistic or surrealistic, and others were abstractions. There were also watercolors of pastoral landscapes. Predominating was a profusion of flowers in vibrant yellow or soothing blue, surrounded by a variety of life-affirming greenery.

Since we were alone, my hard leather shoe heels chuffed on the cork-colored floor. "We're almost there, Faust," I unthinkingly shared with him. At the sound of his name he poked his head out. Looking around, his attention seemed to flit from one painting to another. An oil of a rolling green lawn with massed plantings of in-bloom daffodils fixed his attention. He extended a paw to reach for it. Fortunately, he wasn't close enough to touch it. He extended another paw and mohwed, annoyed at his inability to get close enough. "Shush! We're almost there."

Just then a short, heavy-set woman with tightly-curled, short, dishwater gray hair came out of a room to the left. She was wearing a medium blue smock with the hospice name and logo embroidered on the right breast. The sound re-directed her attention to Faust and his rubbernecking at my back.

"Are you crazy? You can't bring a cat in here!" she nearly shouted, fists on hips, feet apart, aghast at the sight of Faust.

I hadn't heard her rubber-soled shoe steps. Damned sound-dampening, stick-on adhesive tiles. Faust, in turn, laid his ears back and narrowed his amber eyes to creases. He stared aggressively at her as if to say, "We're seeking the Holy Grail. You do anything untoward, like get in our way, Toots, and you'll kiss your fat ass good-bye." Even at moments like this, always a gentleman cat, he refrained from getting as salty as I was wont to do.

I had to think fast. I'd always marveled at how the writers of the *Rockford Files* had Rockford almost instantaneously create characters, scenarios, and actions to handle difficult situations or explain himself. An idea came to mind. It was worth a try. "You must be new here," I deflected her accusation.

She paused, looking confused. "What? Well, yes, but, but what does that have to do with anything? You can't bring that animal in here!" She reasserted her sense of authority.

"Then you may not know about the acceptance of pet therapy in hospices." I was tap-dancing as fast as I could. "Pets are allowed to see their human companions because of the powerful emotional bond between 'owners' and their pets and how their being together reduces patients' anxiety and stress, blood pressure, physical pain, risk of heart attack, loneliness, and depression. A cat's purr, at between twenty and one hundred forty Hertz, is particularly medically therapeutic. It's been shown to also help heal bones as well as muscle and soft tissue injuries."

"I've worked in hospices for years. What in the world are you talking about?"

This caregiver didn't strike me as "offering compassion, hope, and the alleviation of pain and suffering in an environment of support that provides patients with dignity and recognizes their unique needs as well" as the sign out front proclaimed all caregiving teams did. I raised my voice several decibels to almost shouting since I was nearing Room 26. I bellowed, "Alix Brooke really needs to see her cat! Plaaaaay ball!"

The woman looked confused and did a grunting delayed reaction, "Huh? What?"

At that moment, Alix called out, "Here! I'm in here!" Hearing her voice, Faust's ears pricked up and he excitedly struggled to further extricate himself from the knapsack. Once free, he jumped from my shoulder onto the floor. He charged down the hall to her door which was ajar fifteen feet ahead on the left. His claws made muted tinkling sounds on the tiles. The hospice caregiver shuffled after Faust, shouting, "Stop! You can't go in there!"

He ignored her. He was on a sacred quest to see his beloved Alix and had no intention of having it interfered with. He attempted a sliding stop. His rear end slipped sideways, slamming into the far door jamb. Recovering, he raced through the partially-open door of Room 26. There he used a La-Z-Boy recliner in chestnut brown Naugahyde that was positioned at an angle near Alix's bed as a springboard to execute his Olympic four-foot long jump. He landed gingerly beside her blanket-covered, ravaged body.

He paused, looking at his friend. It was as if he were concerned about climbing further onto her body given her fragile, wasted condition. He moved carefully, his back paws missing the surgically-implanted morphine injection pump port, the size of a hockey puck, under the skin of her abdomen. Once under her chin, however, he began licking without hesitation: first her neck, right ear, then her face. He was a cat obsessed, reveling in the unmitigated joy of seeing his "second-best bud" again. He had a lot of loving her to make up for.

Smiling broadly, Alix giggled and chuckled as Faust's whiskers intermittently tickled her nose. She wrapped her arms around him then commenced to kiss and pet his head, scratch between his shoulder blades, and stroke his back all the way to the tip of his tail. He flopped over on his left side and rolled so Alix could stroke his soft tummy. Then she started massaging in front of his ears finally chucking him under the chin for good measure. The two were locked in an unconditional love fest with Faust purring loudly and Alix laughing.

As she lavished her petting, it was hypothesized that the hormones dopamine, oxytocin, prolactin, and serotonin would begin to course through her body. They would increase her Theta waves which would reduce her feelings of anxiety and lift her mood. Faust was her own personal "Dr. Feel Good." It was so heartwarming to hear her almost-hearty from-the-belly laugh again.

The caregiver and I stood in the doorway silently, marveling at this scene. Although it was obvious by her pinched mouth and squinting eyes, the woman was pissed off. But given the tableau before her, she evidentially thought better of saying anything, at least to Alix. And she wasn't going to risk being attacked and ripped to shreds by attempting to remove this strange cat, as if Alix or I would allow her to even try. It was three against one. Alix, who undoubtedly had been depressed, lonely, and nearly zombie-like from her pain-subduing morphine, was suddenly rejuvenated. She looked relaxed, happy, even stronger than her condition would warrant. Vibrant color was returning to her previously ashen face as she smiled at "her" cat.

The mean little kid in me couldn't help wanting to further puncture this so-called caregiver's deflating officious balloon. "See," I offered cheerily, "what the powerful emotional bond between her and her cat has done for Alix." Alix turned her head to smile sweetly at the woman—she even fluttered her eyelashes at her—and nodded. Still annoyed and a little embarrassed, the woman made a point of turning loudly on her rubber heel and leaving in a huff.

Alix and I laughed. "So much for compassion," she whispered. Then, still petting Faust, she directed me to the bedside chair, "What a surprise," she began feigning surprise, "so Faust is *my* cat? You are a clever little devil!" I shrugged, palms up.

As she cradled Faust, I scanned her ten-by-twelve room. It was pleasant with homey touches in its soft blue paint with paisley curtains in dark blue and lavender on a white background on her two windows that looked out onto the colorful plantings. They were open as were the Venetian blinds which covered the windows. She was in a hospital bed with the head slightly elevated. Folded at the foot of the bed, partially covering the cream-colored cotton thermal blanket that was placed on her lower torso, was a floral bedspread in several shades of cool blue.

Beside her bed on the left was an oak nightstand with a lamp, landline telephone, TV remote, a glass and carafe of water in which the ice had mostly melted. On three walls were framed photos of waterfalls, tropical beaches, and horses prancing in a meadow in flower. On the wall opposite her bed was a small oak table with a television set. And between the two windows was a three-drawer oak dresser on which sat her brush and comb, a small radio, and a large vase of lavender and white lilacs in front of a three-by-three decorative oak-framed mirror.

Alix stopped playing with Faust for a moment, pushed the control button to further raise the head of her bed, and said, "Now don't let me forget that I have something else you must promise to do for me. The morphine makes my brain fuzzy so I might not remember. I'm counting on you to remember this for me. You *have* to remember for me. But first I want us to catch up. While I've been tripping the light fantastic at Dana-Farber and here, what and how have you been doing?" Despite her happiness in seeing us, her voice sounded strained and quieter than normal.

I related some of my more interesting coaching

incidents, without breaching client confidentiality, and highlighted some of the articles I had been writing for regional newspapers and national magazines about how social psychology explained much of what was going on in the news. I also mentioned my humorous column on Faust and my trek to the Desert of Maine which had yet to be published. It had been a busy month and a half even while worrying about her. When I finished, I said, "Okay, spit it out. What's the promise?"

Little frown lines appeared between her eyes. "I want you to handle everything after I die." My heart felt like a dropped lead weight. I couldn't breathe. I didn't want to hear her talk about death. "I want you to promise me one thing in particular."

Saliva started filling my mouth. This conversation was making me feel nauseous. I repeatedly swallowed hard and fast.

With a provocative, one-sided grin, she stated, "You must unequivocally promise to bring Faust to my viewing in the funeral home. This is not negotiable. I want him there to say good-bye. I've already arranged for it."

Oh, crap. I balked, "You can't be serious. Faust's being there would likely create a scene. People would be upset, especially since a funeral viewing is supposed to be a solemn occasion. Besides, even though Faust generally likes an audience, I have no way of knowing how he would react to such an unusual situation; you'll be there ... but *deceased*."

"Don't worry. I have confidence in Faust." I

113

wanted to roll my eyes because she must be kidding. "It will be fine," she emphasized, "and I want you *both* there. I want you two to send me off with fanfare."

"Fanfare? What do you mean? If you want 'fanfare,' why not have a wake instead? We could do it at my house or any place you want. We could have food, drinks, music, stories, laughter ... and even some bad puns."

"No. Thanks anyway. I'm having a viewing in a funeral home. No wake. I want Faust to be part of it.

"While I'm having a viewing, I am not having a funeral. I've arranged to be cremated. Then after the viewing ..." Alix eyed me as my anxiety-ridden questions showed on my face and persevered, "I also want you to sprinkle my ashes. I have it all written out for you. I've given the funeral home director explicit instructions, a detailed list spelling out precisely what I want done, when, as well as to expect you and Faust and *not* to interfere with anything you or Faust do."

Teetering in my decision making, I promised her, with an air of resignation, I'd do as she asked. It sounded very risky having Faust there. But if that was what my best friend wanted ... she should have her last wish granted. I was in but I wasn't sure "in" what.

However, the more I thought about her having a funeral home viewing the more puzzled I became. Alix had often expressed that she didn't believe in funerals. In fact, she strongly felt funeral homes shafted people when they were at their most vulnerable. So why have a viewing in a funeral home?

I didn't understand why she was so firm about what she said she wanted and didn't want. Her plans, as she described them, sounded a bit eccentric even for Alix. I wondered if the chemo, cancer, or morphine—or all of the above—could have muddled her thinking a little. But when she finally told me her reason for having a viewing and specifically in a funeral home, I felt stupid. As a psychologist, I felt I should have been able to figure it out even in this overwhelming emotional circumstance.

She reminded me how religious her parents were, even if she wasn't. "They wholeheartedly believed that a funeral represented a public good-bye, a transition between this life and the next. It was expected. No one questioned that everyone in the family would have funerals because it was a given. That was how it had been done in my family for generations.

"But, as you well know, I can't in good conscience have a funeral when I don't believe in them, even in view of my family's persuasion. But still, part of me says I have to respect their beliefs and expectations of me to act in some 'appropriate' fashion, according to their dictates. It doesn't matter that they are no longer alive to see it. So I'm splitting the difference. To be true to myself as well as to them, I'm going to go half way. I'm having a funeral home *viewing*."

Suddenly I mentally slapped my forehead with the heel of my hand. Of course, how could I have been so slow witted. She felt caught between her allegiance to her parents, their beliefs, and desires and her own which were diametrically opposed. She felt a forbiddance about doing something totally against their approval, even at the time of her own death. Their approval was still part of her expectations of herself.

Yeah. I knew only too well about that. Those loyalties, their consequences, and implications that we carry over from childhood can make us contort ourselves into trying to please two masters: our parents, family, and culture AND ourselves. I had been there too as I expected most people had in one way or another. I'd been emotionally loyal to my father who didn't succeed in his field and to myself wanting to succeed in my field. As a result, I would catch myself sabotaging my own efforts so I didn't do better than my father had done.

"Of course, Alix," I said, now enlightened. "You know I'll do whatever you want."

She stressed, "Be sure to read my instructions carefully and follow them strictly. Things may make more sense to you then." She pulled a manila envelope from the night table drawer, smiled mysteriously, and handed it to me.

10

FANFARE WITH A FLOURISH

Faust and I continued to visit Alix every day for at least an hour—even as she increasingly slept through more of the visit from both the devastation of her body and the morphine—until she sank into a deep coma. As I continued to talk to her to let her know I was there, if it might possibly register somewhere within her, Faust spent her last days nestled under her right arm, keeping her warm, comforted, and loved, even when she could no longer respond to him.

In spite of everything I had done leading up to her death, when she died, I wasn't prepared for it. In my mind I had gone through all the steps for dealing with her demise. I wanted to believe that by covering every possible contingency, I could and would meet it head on with that proverbial stiff upper lip. But as a professional, I knew better. Intellectually knowing and expecting something of this significance to happen did not make me ready to accept and deal with it emotionally. I had tried to kid myself before it happened that I had girded my loins like a warrior queen readying herself for battle.

But now every neuron in my body was snapping with the intense, unbearable reality. I felt as if I had been struck by a cement truck going fifty miles per hour which ripped my heart from my body and left me to lie on the side of the interstate to bleed without end. My shattered heart was screaming in anguished pain. Dying so young, the friend who had meant so much to me for so long had been erased from my life, leaving me only with my memories of her. All I wanted was to believe was that it was all a bad dream, that Alix would appear at my door next Wednesday, calling out, "Plaaaaay ball!" I wasn't ready. I felt I never would be.

When Faust and I arrived at the Daniel French Funeral Home in Wayland, Alix's mourners were already gathered in the lobby signing in at Slumber Room Number One. The assembled included her close neighbors, like Claudia and Mara, and her colleagues at Biogen. The number of people present surprised me even though I had let Biogen know and had posted the announcement of her viewing in the *Boston Globe* and *Wayland Town Crier* obituaries. Of course, I wasn't the only one who respected and loved Alix and who would truly miss her.

I was dressed in a light-weight wool navy pants suit with a white silk, long-sleeved blouse, accented by a collar of feline gray fur. Wearing the knapsack for Faust felt tacky for such an occasion. Instead he wore his freshly-washed blue harness and leash and lay quietly around my neck. Being on his best behavior, he seemed to have recognized the need for propriety.

The serious-faced greeter, a heavy-set, sweating man in black, stood at the opening to Slumber Room Number One. He was making sure mourners signed their visitation book. I had no idea why we had to sign—I was tempted not to. I figured that the funeral home was probably going to use the names and addresses for advertising. I could just imagine a glossy four-color, bi-fold brochure and postcard stating, "If you liked Brooke's viewing, don't forget about us when your time has come. No one makes death run more smoothly than Daniel French." Tacky. So tacky.

When he noticed my living neck accessory, he did a double-take before I could introduce myself. He sputtered, looking thunderstruck that I should even consider doing such an unthinkable thing, "You ... you can't bring an animal in here!"

"This is Faust, Alix Brooke's cat. I suggest you speak to your funeral director. He is well aware of Ms. Brooke's last wishes, one of which is to have her favorite cat here today at her viewing."

He began to sweat more profusely and hyperventilate. He looked conflicted about leaving his post. I could envision his systolic blood pressure reading spiking at 200. I pointed in the direction of the director's office. As if retaliating to my offensive digit, he shook his index finger firmly in my face, he stated, "Don't you go anywhere until I get back."

Sure, right, you bumptious turkey. As soon as he hurriedly duck-walked off to find the director, I slipped just inside the open double glass doors and stood there surveilling the scene. Steel folding chairs were lined up six rows of ten in front of the casket on the heavily padded and beige-carpeted floor which was designed to muffle footsteps and voices within the funeral home. Several of the front row seats were filled by elderly funeral-followers, who were dressed in their best funeral attire, with black, old-fashioned pocketbooks hooked on the crook of their elbows. I didn't see anyone who reminded me of "Harold and Maude," but there was time yet, I thought with a grin.

These "followers" were people who daily scoured the obituary columns in the newspapers for services. They were sure to arrive early to secure the front seats and partake of the provided refreshments, which in this case were store-bought cookies and iced tea. I supremely hoped that when I was their age, I'd have better things to do with my time than spend my hours at strangers' viewings and funerals to check out dead bodies, exchange morbid gossip, and snack.

Even though Faust was lying quietly around my neck, his head was rotating 180 degrees as he watched people inside milling around. They were chatting in hushed tones and walking slowly by the departed, nodding, and mumbling things to Alix. Some dabbed their eyes which reminded me I hadn't yet truly cried ... because the tears were still stuck in my throat.

As we finally started up the aisle, passing the

last rows of chairs, a tall, thin man, with sharp features and sparse black hair in a black suit with a crisp white shirt—looking like someone directly out of Central Casting—ran toward me. He had been at the front of the room where he was directing traffic. Trying not to speak too loudly, he blustered, "Wait! Wait! Miss, You can't bring that animal in here!"

"Come on, guys. This is Faust, Alix Brooke's cat. He's specifically expected. I have already sent one of your people to check with your funeral director. As you'll both learn, Ms. Brooke contracted to have this cat at her viewing."

"But, Miss! It's inappropriate. What about the other mourners? You'll upset them."

"Do us both a favor and check it out ... now. And as for the other mourners, I guess they will just have to deal with it however they choose to deal with it. This is what Ms. Brooke unequivocally stated she wanted. It's *her* viewing."

He compressed his lips, furrowed his brow, and race-walked down the aisle and into the lobby. I wondered how many more funeral home staff had not been properly apprised of Alix's wishes. This did not bode well.

We moved slowly past each row. At first, no one paid much attention to us. I was surprised by all the flowers in concrete-looking, white resin urns. Which were what the funeral home provided, for a price, of course, and which were from friends? I'd check the itemized bill when I paid the remainder. Faust, who loved flowers, ignored the purple and white gladiolas, which I doubted Alix would have chosen, but tried to lean close enough to sniff the pink and white carnations. Finding their expected spicy fragrance gone, replaced by hybridized color and the musty aroma of refrigeration, he sneezed twice loudly.

Heads turned at the unexpected, non-human sound. Realizing there was a cat present, surprised mourners started whispering to one another. Three children pointed and giggled. Their parents embarrassedly looked away, shushing them. When that didn't work, they grasped them by the arms and firmly planted them onto their chairs which made the children point and laugh even harder.

The medium-size room was painted a bilious green. Alix would wryly have described it as a cross between "staphylococcal pulmonary exudate" and spearmint. There was white, deep-relief crown molding carved with acanthus leaves every place the purulent walls met the ceiling. In the center of the dark blue night sky ceiling was a white, highly-ornate, plaster Victorian-style floral medallion. At least someone had wisely left off adding stars to the sky.

Music was playing softly. It caught my attention. What was that? It wasn't Bach's "Jesu, Joy of Man's Desiring." It wasn't Pachelbel's "Canon in D." It wasn't even "All Things Bright and Beautiful." Oh, my god! I couldn't believe what I was hearing. How could I have missed Alix's mention of this? It was an organ rendition of "Take Me Out to the Ball

Game." So that was the "fanfare"? Way to go, Alix! Gil Hodges would have been proud.

She really did arrange everything to her particular liking. I'd have loved to have heard the "conversations" she had with the funeral director about that! I could imagine him squirming big time as they tied up the ancillary musical loose ends before signing the contract. He would have been beside himself trying his utmost to convince her that what she ultimately wanted was simply not done, that it was more appropriate to a wake than to a dignified funeral home viewing, especially at prestigious home such as Daniel French.

As I had seen her do before in disagreements, I knew she would have smiled, nodded knowingly, looked him straight in the eye, and unflinchingly responded, "I hear what you're saying. However, it's what I especially want and you've already agreed to take care of the viewing. You have a choice. If you want me to sign the contract, you'll agree."

At that point she would have leaned toward him and patted him on his arm before she continued, "If you no longer care to comply with my wishes, I'll have to look elsewhere. It will cost me time and effort I don't have. But I'm sure I can find another funeral home that's less rigid and more accommodating for my many thousands of dollars." She would pause and look distressed, as if concerned about the effect on the disputant. "It would be a shame to have to tell them why I suddenly needed their assistance on such short notice because of my unnecessarily unpleasant experience here. I understand how competitive the funeral business is."

She would have been good. And how would the funeral director have reacted? What a surprise! Somehow he would have seen the light ... and I don't think it was a "divine" light ... and acceded to the desires of his better, more profitable, angels.

As we approached Alix's body, which I knew was in a wooden box resting inside a fancy rental casket with its split lid open, I noticed, surprisingly, she had "grown" a full right ear. She would have had a small conniption and been insulted and furious that someone had presumptuously "fixed" her right ear. She had explicitly instructed them that nothing be done to *any* part of her, no repairs, no makeup. She wanted simply to appear relaxed in repose. Looking enough like her old self would more than suffice. She didn't want to be made up to look in the peak of health. After all, she was dead.

But funeral home cosmetologists sometimes can't keep their hands off a human canvas, apparently having the "call" to express themselves "artistically." The problem was that sometimes the deceased ended up looking almost like a character out of Mozart's 1791 "The Magic Flute" theatrical production: white-faced, charcoal-eyed, crimson-lipped, round rouged cheeks, with a big black beauty mark, and a wig reminiscent of an unshorn sheep.

Faust leaned over my right shoulder to gaze at

her. At first he seemed unsure. It was his friend lying there but, at the same time, it wasn't. There was none of her magnetic energy being emitted. Still, she was dressed in one of Faust's favorite outfits: a bright red blouse, a hand-woven wool vest in bright blues, yellows, oranges, and crimson, with black slacks which were mostly hidden under the casket's split top.

I could see in the casket by her left shoulder a small, white-tissue-wrapped package with Faust's name on it. Retrieving it, I opened it carefully to see it was a multi-colored silk neck scarf she wore. It had her scent on it. Knowing he'd hold it dear, I slipped it in my pocket to give it to him once we had left. I wasn't sure how he'd respond if I gave it to him there in front of Alix.

It was time. Anxiety twanged my conscience but I had my instructions. Taking a deep breath, I said loudly, "Plaaaaay ball!" Alix's special door-greeting to Faust was his cue. He suddenly leaped from my shoulder and landed spread-eagle over her torso. A mourner in the first row let out a screech in speechless horror as if Dracula had attacked Alix for one last Bloody Mary. The elderly woman clutched her chest then swooned into the arms of a startled seat mate. I felt guilty for her reaction.

Ignoring the noise and theatrics, Faust gently kneaded Alix's upper abdomen with closed eyes, his head down, swaying rhythmically from side to side. He was in his own emotional realm, at one with Alix and with their universe. Slowly he then climbed onto her breast and moved up toward her face which he rubbed with his own. He licked her lovingly, intermittently bunting her cheek before he proceeded toward her right ear as he always did.

Abruptly Faust stopped. He grimaced. Ears back, he pawed at his mouth. The putty holding the wax prosthesis clearly hadn't been able to withstand the pressure of his scratchy tongue. Her fake ear had come off in his mouth. Letting out a guttural mohw, the startled cat rose up, suspended, and spit. Out flew her now-soggy ear attachment. It dropped unceremoniously beside her head. He landed over her chest again, totally bewildered.

The tall, thin man in black ran up behind me, stammering that Faust couldn't do that, "This is a viewing, an unusual one none the less, but a *viewing*! He's desecrating her body!" Faust had already created several rough tire-tread impressions on her cheeks in her carefully-applied mortician's make-up, making her look as if she had been run over by a mountain bike. Ah, well, so much for their desire to give her the "natural look." As Faust moved to pick up the ear prosthesis again, the man foolishly reached into the casket for it as well. I hissed, "No! No! Don't do that! Leave it alone!"

Faust, who recoiled at this stranger's lurch toward him, caught his left front claws in Alix's rented pillow. As the pillow shifted to the right, her head fell to the left, her nose almost buried in the satin-covered padding on that side of her casket. More gasps came from the audience as bystanders couldn't quite decide what to do in such a somber circumstance.

The expressions on some of the elderly freelance mourners' faces spoke volumes. They were fighting to keep their appalled verbal reactions from escaping: "shocking," "incredibly inappropriate," "how dare she," "such impertinence!" But they were in a funeral home, at a viewing, the seriousness and formality of which made them feel self-conscious and stifled about doing anything that might further cause a scene. But some of those present were grinning at the unexpected occurrences.

I tried to push the usher out of the way, saying, "I'll take care of Faust then you can get the ear," but the usher was in his own zone of authoritarian panic. He tried to re-establish the fitting reserve of the occasion by leaning into the casket to pull the pillow into place and carefully re-position Alix's head on it. However, in doing so, his right arm elbowed Faust almost into the closed half of the casket. Faust scrambled to escape, jumping toward the right side and out.

Thinking that this unpredictable, talon-bearing, vampire-toothed wild beast was about to attack him, the stunned usher staggered back. His left shoulder hit the casket lid support. The hinge began to fold. The lid descended. He moved but not fast enough. It slammed onto his shoulder with a thud. He screamed. Stumbling backward, his arm still trapped, he smacked into an urn of freesias. He knocked it sideways. It crashed to the floor, splashing water everywhere. In his attempt to extricate himself with as much dignity as possible, he managed to trample the flower stalks, grinding them into the now-soggy carpet.

Amid the gasps there was hysterical laughter as well rippling through the audience. Undoubtedly Alix's close colleagues had heard about Faust. One man near me chuckled, "Better than a wake. Thanks, Faust, for some comic relief. I like a bit of cabaret with my funeral viewings. It removes some of the holier-than-thou stodginess."

Faust raced down the aisle, through the open double-doors, into the lobby, as if his tail were on-fire. His blue leash trailed behind him, followed by me. I was gobsmacked. I couldn't believe all that had happened. But it was funny ... in a crypt-keeper humorous way. The truth was Alix would have loved it.

The poor cat was hunkered down behind a tall potted *Ficus benjamina* near the front door. Body shaking, head pivoting, he was searching for an exit. He looked not only frightened but also guilt-ridden. I kneeled, gathered him into my arms, and slid onto the carpeted floor to comfort him.

"That was not exactly how either one of us would have expected to have seen her off. However, my friend, none of it was your fault." I was stroking his back to the tip of his tail. "You were a very good kitty. You gave Alix the send-off she wanted. You did your part perfectly." He cocked his head to one side.

"The problems arose because the management didn't follow Alix's instructions." Faust looked up at me at the mention of her name. "They weren't supposed to put make-up on her and they certainly weren't supposed to create a new ear for her." Faust opened his eyes wide as if taking it all in. "That's right. None of that chaos with the usher would have happened if everyone had been informed and followed her instructions precisely." He nodded.

Faust pressed against me and curled up in my lap as his anxiety waned. "Also, you know that aside from a few mourners who were shocked to see a cat at a viewing, especially a cat as 'famous' as you, others seemed to enjoy your presence." Faust looked up at me and lifted his whiskers.

"Alix would have been so proud of you. And I suspect she would have gotten a good belly-laugh over the funeral home-created disaster. I mean she really did go out with a splash—in more ways than one." I laughed.

"Anyway, what do you think about forgetting about refreshments—you don't eat cookies anyway—and just high-tailing it out of here?" I scratched him under the chin and around his ears. He head-bunted me as if to tell me he was ready to go.

With his frayed nerves soothed, I put him on the carpet to take up his leash. He looked up at me and did a wobbly pirouette of sorts on his hind legs as he sank slightly into the plush. "That's beautiful. I'm sorry you didn't get a chance to do that for Alix one more time." He did another dip. "Ready?" Faust mohwed. I rose from my sitting position. "Okay, let's go." As we walked through the front doors, he briefly looked back, almost longingly, as if a final gesture to Alix.

11

RISING FROM THE ASHES

I was glad the viewing was out of the way. Next came the scattering of her ashes. As the one appointed to attend to all matters funereal after she died, I had had to make sure her body was properly transported to the funeral home, that the viewing was arranged, the cremation scheduled and done, her ashes retrieved, and then scattered where requested. The process had turned out to be not as straightforward or uncomplicated as I had expected.

While the home did pick up her body from hospice and ferry it over to the funeral home, the funeral home manager tried to convince me that I needed to purchase a real split mahogany, satin-lined casket for the viewing. As per Alix's arrangements, she had already contracted to rent from them a casket with a removable interior. Because she was going to be cremated, she had purchased a simple, fully combustible wood-like container to be placed into the casket. The resulting appearance was that she was lying in the expensive mahogany, satin-lined casket. When dealing with the funeral home before the viewing, my reinforcing Alix's decisions visibly irritated the manager.

"Look," I finally said with more than a little bit of sarcasm. "I personally don't care if we rent the casket for the afternoon or have her propped up in a chair as if holding court. I have Alix's signed contract and all the agreed-upon instructions. As I'm sure you know, changing your mind is not an option at this juncture. Therefore, I expect you to just abide by the contract and her instructions."

The funeral home manager sat there, across his ornate, highly-polished rosewood desk from me, his teeth clamped together and his lips pursed into an anal pucker. His hands were clasped so tightly his knuckles looked like snowcaps. Clearly he was annoyed and exasperated. Tough stuff, Bozo.

Following that was the controversy over her ashes. The funeral home didn't want to release them to me in anything other than one of their expensive brass urns. Well, actually, they allowed that it could also be in one of their expensive marble, jade, silver, gold, or platinum urns which came in varying sizes from twelve inches to twenty-four, or even larger if I wished to "place it on a pedestal in my foyer." They indicated that the ashes had to be transferred to me in something "suitably funereal."

I wanted to say, that's meadow muffins, dude. You may be talking to the bereaved, but I didn't just parachute in. I wanted to say that you're supposed to sound empathetic not greedy. You're talking about a signed-sealed-delivered contract so knock off the crummy sales pitch. Your manipulation is royally pissing me off. Just because I haven't as yet paid the remainder of your exorbitant but agreed-upon bill, doesn't mean you can keep trying to add to it. If you want to be paid, not sued, do as you contracted to do, you grasping creeps!

Of course, what I actually said was less confrontational. I was, after all, a professional who coached people in effective interpersonal communication, dealing with conflict, overcoming obstacles, solving problems, and reaching goals. So I said, "Since the ashes are to be scattered, *not* displayed on some mantelpiece, as Alix has already indicated, I want you to place them in a plastic bag and place the bag into the Chock full O'Nuts can I'm supplying."

It didn't seem to matter what they had already agreed to. This cremation staff person wasn't the least bit pleased with my "insensitive" choice for the ashes. As far as I was concerned, that was just too damned bad. That was his problem. He could agonize about it with his analyst.

It's funny what can thread through your mind at the strangest times. While this person was huffing and puffing, I was hearing in my head the Chock full O'Nuts jingle: "Chock full O'Nuts is a heavenly coffee … a better coffee a millionaire's money can't buy," sung by Page Morton Black, the wife of the coffee company owner. It transported me to my teenage years when the black-and-white commercial was frequently shown on Boston television, well before the death of a close friend and this funeral home had entered my life. Lost in my reverie, I smiled, even as the cremation staff person glowered at me, becoming angrier that I was obviously not taking this issue seriously.

After trying a little harder to chastise, shame, and humiliate me for what he perceived as my "bad taste," he unwillingly agreed. Of course, he agreed. He had no choice. What a clown! I wrote a check for the remainder of the bill with the funds Alix had provided me for it. My only concern and hope at that point was that what I would receive were indeed her ashes and not cement dust.

Perhaps I had read too much Stephen King. But after all this contention, I had visions of the funeral home dumping Alix's body in a landfill to save on the cost of firing up the burners in the cremation chamber's retort to 1,800 degrees Fahrenheit and then troweling ashes from someone's fireplace to fill their high-priced human-ash-remains receptacles.

Of course, in reality, it was what it was, except as a legal matter of potential fraud. These individuals didn't strike me as the most trustworthy of business people. However, I was not about to have a laboratory do an analysis of the can's purported contents.

As if to put the cherry on the top of this sundae, when the staff person "presented" me with the plastic bag in the coffee can, he gingerly conveyed it to me as if it were a not a lead-lined container of radioactive cat excrement.

I had to laugh. How could they be so terminally

stupid? Didn't they know that a bad experience with a service, especially one so intimate and devastatingly emotional, spreads by word of mouth like a wildfire. That's exponentially faster than a good experience with one. The keystone of marketing is that "perception is everything." This funeral home didn't need karma to bite them in the butt sometime in the future. They were doing a great job all by themselves in the here and now.

Late the next day Faust and I drove out to 915 Walden Street in Concord to visit the Walden Pond reservation. Surrounding us were the 2,680 lush acres of Walden Woods, comprised of American elm, American ash, red oak, paper birch, and staghorn sumac. As requested, we were to perform Alix's final ritual at the beginning of sunset. Somehow that seemed to me to make the atmosphere of one of her favorite locations even more transcendental.

As we walked the trail to the pond's edge, we passed a large horizontal wood sign, painted dark brown with white incised words of Thoreau: "I went to the woods because I wished to live deliberately, to front only the essential facts of life, and see if I could not learn what it had to teach, and not, when I came to die, to discover that I had not lived." Next to the sign stood granite stones which outlined the area where his tiny house had stood. From there it was two hundred feet to the water's edge.

Faust, wearing his blue harness and leash, was draped around my neck as I stepped toward the 102-foot-deep pond's kettle-hole shoreline. In my right hand was a tote bag holding the lidded coffee can of Alix's ashes and her dog-eared paperback copy of Henry David Thoreau's *Walden: Or Life in the Woods*. In it I had marked passages I felt most appropriate to read. Alix had left that choice to me.

I removed the can with my left hand, placed it on the ground, near a high-bush blueberry. Then I grabbed the book, letting the tote drop to the smooth earth with a resounding plop. "Ready, Faust?" I asked as I opened the yellowing book to its paper-clipped pages and read as twilight approached.

"A single gentle rain makes the grass many shades greener. So our prospects brighten on the influx of better thoughts. We should be blessed if we lived in the present always, and took advantage of every accident that befell us, like the grass which confesses the influence of the slightest dew that falls on it."

"All change is a miracle to contemplate, but it is a miracle which is taking place every instant."

"I learned this, at least, by my experiment: that if one advances confidently in the direction of his dreams, and endeavors to live the life which he has imagined, he will meet with a success unexpected in common hours."

"I have, as it were, my own sun and moon and stars, and a little world all to myself."

As I finished reading, I put the book in the tote for safekeeping and lifted Faust off my shoulders.

After placing him at the water's edge, I secured the ashes' receptacle. Removing the plastic snap-off lid, I held the can high and proclaimed, "Alix, Here is to your true simplicity and solitude, to your large, loving heart and sweet soul. You are forever in our thoughts and lives. You've always been the very best friend. And, as always, kiddo, 'Plaaaaay ball!'" I sprinkled the ashes into the redolent air, some fluttering onto the water's deepening purple surface while others landed softly on the soil.

Faust who had been watching ducks fly overhead now watched as the grit and flakes floated down like fire flies against the deepening pink and tangerine sky. He began to jump to catch them with his paws and tongue, inadvertently stepping into the water. He shook each foot independently to remove the excess moisture. I smiled as he played with Alix one last time ... until a piece of ash landed directly on his tongue. Crinkling his nose, he began to spit. I put my hand to my mouth to stifle a laugh. "Okay, it's time."

Back on my shoulders, he sniffed the air with a wonder I hadn't observed before, nuzzled my neck, and gave me a little love nip on the cheek. Returning the can to the tote and with the tote in hand, we slowly walked back through the trees, with their leaves forming a ceremonial canopy. Only the luckiest and brightest stars displayed their scintillations through the vault of branches for Alix's valediction.

The following day reality finally struck with a

vengeance. I could no longer use following Alix's every instruction to the letter to keep it together. That was done ... and so was I. Starting in the morning with a few sniffs, it progressed to my lying curled up in a fetal position on my bedspread with Faust at my side, kneading me. Eyes red and puffy, I cried unabatedly, and asked the universe, "Why?"

A few days later when clearing out her house, I discovered Alix had left me a large box containing folders of my letters to her and her pertinent papers. These had since been sitting by my desk for weeks awaiting my perusal. As I began thumbing through the folders of the mass of correspondence which went back decades, I saw copies of short stories I had written in my younger years and a completed novel-to-be.

"Faust, most of these writings never saw the light of publishing, thanks be to the Cosmic Muffin." Faust stepped off one of the folders where he had been sitting and curled around my neck.

My first attempt at a novel in particular caught my eye. How old was it? Twenty years? ... When I was so young. As I turned the cover page, the writing held my attention. It was like a car accident. I couldn't look away. So I forced myself to read the first couple of pages, aloud, to Faust. "Promise you won't laugh," I cautioned.

Chapter 1

Caitlin O'Shaughnessey lunged forward, her sweating palm on the bannister rail. The heavily varnished wood was slick. Her lithe body doubled over as her stocking feet raced to meet head and arms. Panting, she halted and squinted down into the abysmal stairwell. Before her was a black hole, pulling her down into its inkiness. Her mind spun. Where? Where could she turn? she asked herself. Her seafoam green eyes searched for a door or window. Salty sweat ran down her glowing face. It burned her eyes as she teared and strained to perceive a glimmer of light.

"She's my alter ego," added Mo Higgins as she placed her spiral notebook back on her lap. "By the way," she chuckled, "you can include that in my clinical history: Multiple Personality Disorder." She waited for the psychotherapist to respond to Mo's introduction to her seventh romantic suspense novel.

"I see. Journalist heroine Caitlin O'Shaughnessey is once again on the brink of danger, dangling over the precipice. Tell me, Maureen, to what degree do you feel like Caitlin?" asked Zoe Wescott, Ph.D., as the 50-year-old clinical psychologist rolled her wheelchair to the side of her teak desk to be closer to Mo.

"Please call me Mo. You mean on the brink of danger? Me? No. That's just how each of my six previous books starts—you know, with a big dramatic moment. Then I use a flashback to tell how Caitlin has gotten there, before resuming the action. It's just a formula I use. Then I substitute different situations, characters, and motivations. In this way I don't have to reinvent the wheel each time. Call it paint-by-the-numbers or connect-the-dots, if you will, but my audience likes the fantasy and excitement. And this means I can put Caitlin anywhere, in any situation, like in a British castle escaping from IRA gun-runners, in a Southern mansion eluding a white supremacist group, or in a Boston tenement trying to outwit Colombian drug dealers."

Dr. Wescott continued, "I'd like to talk about what you see as your problem—what brought you here. You indicated that you've felt 'on edge' for a long time. It sounds to me like Caitlin's not the only one hanging over that edge."

"There's no resemblance between me and Caitlin." Mo shook her head, frowning. "Caitlin is 25, statuesque, paper-thin but 'voluptuous'—you know those physical contradictions that symbolize 'beauty' these days. She has flowing raven tresses, no bad hair days, a well-paying job. I, on the other hand, am 34, five-two, a size 12, have frizzy red hair, glasses, and pull in $20,000 annually for sitting behind a typewriter eighty hours a week, churning out slick pulp for a fickle reading audience. The only thing about me that's dangling at the moment is my flesh."

"You sound angry with yourself. Don't you like who you are?" Wescott looked straight into Mo's eyes. Mo wriggled in her chair.

"Me angry? I'm just your average middle-aged American female. Of course, by Hollywood standards, my breasts are too small, my butt is too big, and my jawline is undefined. And unlike screen actresses whose most important anatomy is always 'at-attention,' even in repose, when I lie on my back, my breasts flatten out and slide into my armpits. Why wouldn't I like myself?"

Mo paused, reflecting. "Okay, sure, I'm pissed. At everyone and everything." Mo waved a dismissive hand. "It probably started when I found out I was different from little boys," she joked, remembering a line Celeste Holm spoke in the film *All About Eve*. She shook her head, smiled, then let her gaze drift toward the ceiling. As her smile vanished, she picked up her notebook and read another passage.

Caitlin shook her head to clear her mind. The height and darkness affected her judgment. She secured her left hand on the rail in front of the charging right. Her heart pounded rapidly and her head began to swim. "No," she screamed unheard, "not now. I must get away." Her shoeless feet felt the shocking coldness of large-headed nails in the steps. Peeling paint curled between her toes and abrasively brushed her calves as she resumed her slow descent.

As I put the manuscript down on the desk, Faust climbed off my shoulders and went to his litter box. "I heard that comment, Mister!" I said laughing. "I can't believe Alix saved this. It's so ... so ... uh ... over the top."

I could laugh now but when I wrote it, I was so earnest, pouring my inexperienced literary heart out, so sure I was going to capture romance suspense fiction by storm ... be snapped up by a top-level Manhattan romance publisher, instead of the small publisher I used ... and be on the *New York Times* best-seller list for an indeterminate number of months. Mo Higgins and Caitlin O'Shaughnessy would be household names.

But, good grief, at that time I didn't have a clue about writing a book. Yet for years I sent Alix chapters and other samples of my work. In response she pointed out my strengths, when she could find them, and questioned me about what I intended to convey by some word, phrase, or sentence. She always encouraged me to read as much as I could, see how published authors structured their stories and what worked and didn't work for me as a reader in their books. But most importantly she stressed I should just keep working at it, writing all the time and refining and refining. It was surprisingly astute advice from a non-writer.

Before I put the manuscript back into its folder, I noticed a yellow Post-It note sticking out from between the back pages. It said, "Great start. Keep writing! Learn! NEVER give up!" signed "A." My eyes welled up. She had always been there for me.

12

MR. MITTEN'S SECRET WEAPON

Weeks went by as Faust and I resumed our regular schedules. We bicycled around the neighborhood in the morning before breakfast, with him wearing his harness and leash, wrapped around my shoulders. Afterward, I worked on an upcoming seminar on how best to use networking in order to accomplish any goal for yourself and help others or coached a client on the phone. In the meantime, Faust contemplated the state of the world by lying on my desk, looking over his stomach through his hind legs as he fastidiously groomed himself.

When I first took him out to ride with me—years ago—I had made the inexcusable error of securing Faust into the bike's basket. Unable to move as he expected and feeling trapped, he tried to escape. As a result, he toppled the bicycle, nearly becoming pancaked underneath it. Somehow neither of us was physically injured though I wasn't sure about what trauma he might have endured. The incident impressed upon me that I needed to remember to consult with Faust first and not simply assume he'd go along with whatever I had in mind for him. I had to admit that we humans tend to be egocentric, and even arrogant, especially when dealing with nonhumans.

This morning as we started along Willow Road, there was a little girl at the side of the road crying. It was Julie, who lived five houses down from us. Beside her on the grassy edge was the body of a black and white kitten, looking to be about thirteen weeks old. Sobbing, she said she had just found it and was sure it was dead. We stopped about six feet from her, I set the kick stand, and I walked over to her where I put Faust on the grass beside me.

"Any idea what happened to the kitten, Julie?" I asked as I began gently touching the baby, looking for blood and broken bones. She shook her head. I surmised it was abandoned, feral, or lost. The kitten wasn't dead but it was unconscious and breathing shallowly. No blood or foam appeared at its mouth or nose. Its mouth and airway looked clear. No nose or eye exudate. There were no wounds or abscesses on its body. Its legs, spine, head, and rib cage all seemed intact. "It might be ill or stunned," I stated, guessing, as I slowly moved its front legs to see if I could rouse it. It roused itself imperceptibly.

Julie hovered over the kitten, tears still slipping down her cheeks, and asked tentatively, "Will it be okay?"

"Maybe. It doesn't appear hurt. But, if it's okay with you, I'll take him home to check him out." Julie nodded. I carefully placed the kitten in the bike's basket. I put Faust, who had been looking on with concern, back on my shoulders.

"Oh, yes. Oh, yes. Can I come with you too?"

"Of course, but first go tell your mom you want to come with me to see if we can help the kitten."

When she raced back out of her house, she trotted in behind my bicycle as I walked it back home. Faust was craning his neck to watch the kitten, seemingly intent upon its state of health, as if he were trying to solve this medical puzzle. Once I had parked the bicycle in the single-car garage attached to my rented house, I carried the little ball of fluff into the kitchen.

While Julie gently held the kitten, I collected a hand towel from the bathroom and a heating pad from the linen closet. On the counter near the sink I placed the half-folded towel on the heating pad I had set on "low." Julie handed the black and white kitten to me. Fortunately, Julie's mother had given her daughter a quart of milk to bring along for the kitten. I didn't have any—Faust and I didn't drink milk. And I didn't have any KMR, kitten milk replacer. Julie had put the bottle on the round cherry wood kitchen table.

Constantly checking the temperature, I warmed a quarter-cup of milk which I drew into an unused eyedropper I kept wrapped in a napkin in the utility drawer near the sink. As I talked softly to the kitten, I waved the milk-filled eyedropper under its nose. The kitten responded to the smell, opened its eyes, moved its head to look around, and stretched its legs slightly. I placed a drop of milk on its lips. Suddenly an eager, little pink tongue grabbed it.

Drop by drop the kitten sucked in the liquid. After ingesting nearly the whole eye dropper, it began, with some difficulty, to raise its upper body and look around. It was a male, looking to be at least three months old, half-way to adolescence.

Julie clapped her hands, repeating, "The kitten's going to be okay. The kitten's going to be okay. He's going to be my kitten. My kitten!"

"He'll need to be checked out by a veterinarian to make sure he's really okay. And then he'll need some kitten shots to protect him." I didn't bother going into additional details about testing the kitten for feline-leukemia virus and de-worming him.

Continuing to feed the baby, I switched to a little of Faust's canned food instead of milk. Cow's milk isn't good for cats in general and could give the baby diarrhea. As I conversed with Julie, Faust was sitting on the floor below the kitten. He was flipping his tail back and forth, smacking the gray linoleum. With attending to the kitten I hadn't been paying attention to him. Suddenly he ascended as if by jetpack onto the counter beside the kitten. The kitten looked up at Faust with wide, pale green eyes. As Faust leaned over him, my heart stopped. Had he ever seen a kitten before? How would he feel about it?

But I should have known better. Faust began gently licking the kitten's head, ears, and face. The kitten rolled over and Faust groomed his tummy and whole body. As this was going on, I had Julie watch them to make sure the kitten didn't slip too

146

close to the counter's edge as I called Dr. Bridges for an appointment for the kitten. The first available was three o'clock the next day.

When I returned, Julie began excitedly dancing around the kitchen, singing, "He's my kitten ... my kitten. I'm going to have a kitten."

"I hope that's true. But in the meantime you need to go home to talk to your mother about the kitten. Please tell her she can call me if she has any questions."

"You'll take care of Mr. Mittens for me?"

"Julie, 'Mr. Mittens' is a great name. He will go to the veterinarian tomorrow afternoon to make sure he is healthy or if he needs any medicine. I'll let you know what she says. Okay?"

Julie nodded.

"You head back home now. And thank your mother for the milk. The kitten doesn't need any more of it and can eat canned kitten food which I'll pick up for him."

With the quart of milk in her hands, Julie unenthusiastically left for home. The kitten lolled and stretched at Faust's touch. By evening the kitten's temporary bed was situated in the bathroom. It was walking around, sharing canned food with Faust, and checking out the fresh litter pan. The kitten was playing with Faust who was exceedingly gentle with his little companion. Faust was also encouraging the kitten to try different activities. The kitten, which was already neurologically almost at his adult level, was pouncing, climbing, and jumping around. His athleticism, grace, and confidence suggested Mr. Mittens was going to be one well-coordinated and active cat.

When the kitten became sleepy, Faust directed the kitten to his own kitty bed in the bedroom, which he now rarely used since he slept with me. Together they curled up as if they had always been best friends. Perhaps not so surprisingly, when I headed into bed, Faust didn't join me. Instead, he stayed with the kitten as if keeping him warm, protecting him from the demons of the night, and providing him with the comfort and love only another of his species could provide.

The next day Dr. Bridges found the kitten to be in good health overall. She tested for feline leukemia virus, which was negative, de-wormed him, and gave him his first kitten shots. Today he looked perky and ready to take on the world. Faust stayed in the carrier with him. He was probably giving him his first lessons in what every young male cat should know. On the way home I stopped at Julie's house to give her the good news and let her pet Mr. Mittens.

At that time her mother was close-mouthed about the kitten. It was hard to see what she thought about having him in the household. But when she frowned and bit her lip, her conflict was obvious. She guided me into the next room while Julie played on the floor with the kitten.

"I don't know about having a cat," she shared. "I don't like them. I mean I've never had one. It's not that I ever had a bad experience with one. I mean a cat never scratched me or scared me or anything like that. But cats seem so watchful, you know, watching everything you do. It's like they're judging you. It seems so creepy. And they seem so mean, you know, being hunters, killers of birds. I'm not saying they're evil but they're sly and manipulative."

"Would you be willing at least to meet Mr. Mittens ... for Julie's sake? She is very smitten with him."

"All right, but 'meeting' him just for Julie's sake."

I called Julie to bring Mr. Mittens into the den. The moment the kitten saw Julie's mother, he reached out his white-stockinged front paws. Julie held the kitten closer to her mother. Mr. Mittens reached out again. Julie's mother bent down. The kitten gently touched her face and leaned toward her to lick her nose. The woman smiled, seemed to luxuriate in the tickling touch of this baby. But, suddenly, she pulled back, as if Tasered by her long-held belief that shouted, "No! Don't! That's fraternizing with the enemy."

I said to Julie, "I'm going to keep the kitten for the next ten days just to make sure we've covered everything and he's doing okay." Then I asked her mother, "At that time do you think you might give Mr. Mittens a trial run? Maybe for two weeks?" Julie's mother didn't respond. She ran her tongue over her lips. I continued, "If you let Mr. Mittens come stay with you for that brief period, you can feel free to call me with any questions you have about his care or behavior. And then, after that time, if you truly believe it's not working out, I could take him."

As I was saying these things, I was thinking what if they didn't bond? While I respected the no-kill animal rescue shelters in the area, I didn't want to take him to one of them where he'd have to go every week to adoption clinic which could be so discouraging and stressful. That meant I'd have to provide the baby with a permanent home. But that also meant it would no longer be Faust and I alone. We had been a team, inseparable, since this diseased, walking feline skeleton had found me and maneuvered me into taking him to my bosom.

While Faust had generously, at the outset, shown his nurturing side to the helpless kitten, he might not be interested in sharing the limelight into the future. Ever since we met, he had been *the* center of attention. If the kitten joined us, that situation would no longer be the case. They would share everything, including me.

But then, I realized, I wasn't just concerned about Faust. I was also concerned about me. I would no longer be the center of Faust's world. That felt like a huge loss. As much as I was willing to help the kitten and adopt him if necessary, I wanted Julie's mother to accept and begin to really care for Mr. Mittens. Julie needed a Mr. Mittens in her young life, to learn from, love, and be loved in return. As I waited for an answer from Julie's mother, Julie looked at her fervently with hopeful expectation.

After ten days when Mr. Mittens was doing well and getting stronger, Julie's mother acceded to having the kitten join their household for two weeks *only*. She didn't seem overjoyed about the prospect, however, but did it for Julie's sake. But it's funny how things don't always work out the way you might expect.

Julie's alleged "cat hating" mother quickly discovered that the kitten thought she walked on water, healed lepers, and changed water into wine. Specifically, Mr. Mittens slept with Julie's mother, totally eschewing the cat bed I had lent Julie. He'd sit by her mother's bed at bedtime, mew to be pulled up onto the bed, and then he'd cuddle against her chest. During the day he followed her everywhere, rubbing against her legs, and snuggled into her lap purring loudly whenever she sat for even a moment.

Cats are smart. Even at his young age, Mr. Mittens was very savvy about taking advantage of every opportunity to ingratiate himself with the person he thought mattered most for his survival. By the end of fourteen days, the little tuxedo kitten had so insinuated himself into Julie's household that there was no way in heaven or hell he would be asked to leave. In fact, I had the strong impression that Julie's mother, who was cuddling with the kitten when I visited, would have fought like a mama tiger to keep him there. That was precisely how my mother had become a cat aficionado.

Julie was so thrilled that she would have her furry companion, one who was now beginning to spend his nights split between Julie and her mother. As a result, she promised me faithfully that Mr. Mittens would be an indoor cat so he couldn't run into the road or be hurt by a dog wanting to play. She also swore she would keep his litter pan clean and make sure he always had fresh water available and scheduled meals of kitten chow and canned kitten food. He wouldn't be shifting into adult cat food until he was about one year old.

Because she wanted Mr. Mittens to be like Faust and walk on a leash, I gave her red harness and leash for when Mr. Mittens was a little older—he was already growing fast. Included with the harness were my positive-reinforcement instructions about how to train him and the promise that one day we four could walk Willow Road together. Glowing, she acted as if Santa Claus had given her carte blanche on anything she wanted for the rest of her life.

During the first days of Mr. Mittens' two-week trial at Julie's, Faust walked around the house looking for the kitten. At first he seemed a little confused and distraught that he couldn't find him. He wouldn't dance for me either spontaneously or when asked to. He slept in his kitty bed he had shared temporarily with Mr. Mittens. But as the days passed, he melted into his former routine of sleeping with me, following me around, dancing, catching and throwing the Wiffle Ball, and lavishing me with all his attention.

A twinge of guilt stabbed me. Maybe he should have a friend of his own species as well. Maybe I was being selfish in making me his one and only companion. On second thought, maybe not. After all he had likely been through in his early life, he needed and deserved my full-time attention ... and I, his.

13

A RENTAL FROM HELL

Not long after Mr. Mittens became a permanent fixture in Julie's home, I received a letter from the owners of my house, Tom and Molly Ansel. I'd known Tom for many years when I worked at Massachusetts Institute of Technology's Mechanical Engineering Department on a textile thesaurus project for the U.S. Bureau of Standards. He was with IBM and consulted on that project. They were returning from Europe in about two months because Tom's promotion was bringing them back.

When they first knew they were being transferred overseas, Tom suggested I house-sit for them for however long they'd be gone. That was a wonderful offer but I insisted on paying some kind of rent, if only as a token. Paying that minimal amount plus the utilities enhanced my bank account. As I began scouring the houses-for-rent pages in the *Sunday Boston Globe*, I saw an ad for a cleaning product for cat stains. That triggered an uncomfortable recollection.

When I signed the so-called "rental agreement" with the Ansels, they were talking effusively about the neighborhood on Willow Road. Molly had mentioned all the beautiful cats—some residents but others undoubtedly lost or abandoned—that tried to visit them but that she couldn't pet or adopt because of her allergy to cat dander. At that time Faust hadn't as yet cornered and mesmerized me into becoming his companion. But now? After his several years at the house, I would really have to do a super job of scrubbing every inch of the house to erase, as much as was humanly possible, nearly every singular molecule of evidence of Faust's having lived there. That meant especially the upholstery, draperies, and rugs. No good deed goes unpunished.

So when I was not cleaning, writing articles for newspapers and magazines, doing seminars, or seeing clients, I was on the look-out for something interesting to rent. My ideal was a small, single-family home with a garage, trees, and a small garden, something that was not too expensive. Prominent in my mind was that it should not be new construction. I'd been there and done than ... and had no wish to repeat the experience.

At one time, I had craved living near the ocean. I had never lived near water but found the prospect delicious. I wanted to watch the waves and hear the roar as they rolled in and slapped Massachusetts' rocky coastline. Serendipitously, as I scanned the "Apartments for Rent" in the Sunday *Boston Globe*, I saw a nearly new apartment building at the very tip of Bass Point in Nahant, just across the causeway from Lynn, a city north of Boston. Nahant was a one-mile square island that jutted out into

Massachusetts Bay. It was a residential community and summer resort historically linked to Henry Wadsworth Longfellow. There were no state roads in town, just a single main street. I knew it would be so picturesque and inviting.

The over-100-unit, two-story apartment complex which was now just a few years old, had one vacant five hundred square-foot, one-bedroom apartment on the second floor. I called the on-site management office then headed to the North Shore. On the eastern Massachusetts map this area of Nahant stood out, humorously, like a flaccid phallus. And Sea Breeze Lane, on which the apartment complex sat, looked anatomically like its urethra, running its full length. In retrospect, maybe that should have told me something. The exterior of the apartment complex buildings was gray-blue vertical wood siding with dark blue trim. They looked very Nantucket nautical without the artificial seaside embellishments. The manager met me in front of the building.

The apartment was up one flight of stairs, with a galley kitchen to the immediate right with butcher-block counters and a window over the sink looking out onto the parking lot, a bedroom with two windows facing the ocean, and large, beige-carpeted living room-dining room combination with wide sliding-glass doors facing the water. An over-sized walk-in closet in the dining area, against the kitchen wall, could fit a typing table, typewriter, and small book shelves to serve as my office. I was working on a programmed text entitled *Decision*

Making for Managers for AMACOM, the American Management Association book division.

A side door to the right of the living room on this end building opened directly onto a gray-painted wooden staircase down to the small grassy area between buildings, just short of the boulder-strewn shore. Outside the apartment, through the glass doors was a dark blue-painted wood balcony nearly over the ocean where if I leaned out far enough, I might, if I were lucky, catch some invigorating salt spray.

Because of its location jutting out into the Atlantic, it had splendid views. Southwest was Logan Airport in Boston, the city of Winthrop's Belle Isle Marsh and Reservation, and the high-rises of Boston proper. More southerly was Boston Harbor's Island National Recreation Area. I loved its immediate connection with raw Nature, where I could sit on the rocks below and become one with the crisp breezes, waves, and ocean's beckoning jet engine. I coveted it and wanted it more than any other place I had ever seen. Despite my overarching desire to simply snatch it up, I carefully inspected the apartment and lease then I signed. That was before I had met Faust in Sudbury which was probably just as well because the apartment complex was designated "No Pets Allowed."

I moved into the apartment in early fall which gave me time to create some heavy, lined, floor-length draperies of orange-rust burlap for the wonderful wall of glass to cut down heat loss on cold nights. Everything was idyllic until the fall winds began to violently blow off the water. Suddenly I found I couldn't maintain the temperature in the apartment. When the gusts rattled the glass doors, the draperies fluttered, and I felt at risk for frostbite.

As the outside temperatures dropped, I awoke to a fifty-five-degree apartment. Wrapping my chilled body snugly in my old red Eastern Mountain Sport down coat, I would walk into the living room to see the bottom of the heavy drapes rolled upward by the wind. Pushing aside the fabric, I watched the locked glass doors and their single screen door flex, making a harsh scraping and squeaking sound in the gusts. A jet stream curled around their steel frame. With my down coat on top of the bedspread I tried to get back to sleep.

As soon as the sun rose the next day, I called the management company to explain what I deemed a "significant problem." To my considerable annoyance, my concern and complaint were cavalierly dismissed. Unfortunately, this was not the first time I had had this difficulty. Frequently men didn't seem to listen to me, much less believe me, as I explained in detail a problem that needed to be solved. What usually happened was they acted as if I were exaggerating. Sadly, this wasn't a situation that was unique to me. Women's concerns often tended to be discounted and dismissed.

The management representative said he'd have someone come by the following week. I said I needed them sooner, that the thermostat couldn't maintain a livable temperature at night. But that fact obviously had no impact. I could hear him stifle a laugh. Feeling impotent, I was livid. Even though I requested he look for himself, he chose not to check out my claim.

In the interim, I located a carpet company across the causeway in Lynn. From them I purchased heavy industrial-strength plastic sheeting for window insulation which I taped around the glass wall using double-sided pressure-sensitive tape. This was before the advent of heat-shrink plastic. They also had rolls of old, used, green rubber carpet padding that I could have. I envisioned placing them at the foot of the glass doors, against the draperies to stifle cold air movement.

Lugging these two heavy, five-foot-wide rolls up the stairs to my apartment took more time than I had imagined. Shreds of dried green rubber decorated the stairs as well as my carpet in monster-truck-like tracks. Once I rolled them into the living room, I shoved them firmly against the base of the draperies and the glass behind them. But that night as the coastal spirits keened warnings of an impending death in the house, no doubt from hypothermia, the winds seeped in, rippled the draperies, and circulated around the rolls. The living room thermometer went into another nose dive.

When the two men from management finally arrived, it was late in the day. They may have done this purposely to indicate their low level of concern. But, in fact, it actually worked to my benefit. They looked at the large green rolls and laughed as if I had done it to be theatrical. Their inspection was cursory and they shook their heads and heaved a sigh as if to reinforce their disbelief. "Sorry, little lady," they said looking down at me, "it simply couldn't possibly happen like you said."

That stimulated my adrenaline. As I explained again in brief physical detail how the door glass flexed in the wind, they all but rolled they eyes as if importuning a supreme being to save them from this nonsense. Then they threw in the kicker that was supposed to put this obviously "hysterical female" in her place: "No one else has ever complained about the doors having a problem or not being properly installed!"

Bad move, guys. As I gritted my teeth, I thought you're pulling that manipulation crap on the wrong "little lady." Flexing my knees, throwing back my shoulders, and setting my feet and jaw firmly, I said, "I don't care if no one else has ever had this problem before. *I* have this problem now and *I* want you fix it by properly by installing new doors."

They seemed surprised at my declaration. They were about to argue with me further when the fast-approaching-winter gusts started to flex the glass. Quickly I rolled away the rubber carpet padding and pulled aside the drapes. The glass looked as if it were a human chest hyperventilating. The blast distributed itself around the door frame, causing even these two who had already taken off their coats, to involuntarily shiver. They mumbled between themselves, looking disgruntled, then stated, "Of course, we'll have to charge you for the labor."

I wanted to laugh at their cheek. "No," I said, not letting my facial muscles demonstrate my incredible disbelief, "you're mistaken. I'm *not* paying for *your* poor building construction. That's *your* problem and *your* fix. I expect you to replace the ill-fitting glass doors, frames and all ... at *no* cost to me."

Threats weren't necessary at that point. I didn't need to mention possibly putting my rent in escrow or suing them. In two days they did the job. Starting early in the day, they finished before dusk. The rest of the winter was much warmer and cozier.

However, that wasn't the end of my ocean-hugging apartment problems. Consequently, over the next several months the building super and I became much friendlier than I would have preferred. Repeatedly the toilet would clog and overflow, which was not the result of anything I was doing—if you discount my simply using it as expected. It appeared that there was a glitch in their plumbing installation too. I wondered if the former occupants—assuming anyone else had stayed here long—had enjoyed contending with these recurring problems. It was not for me to learn if the pipes ran up instead of down, made ninety-degree turns, or had an obstruction in them.

As much as my mouth had watered over having

an apartment overlooking the ocean, I now had to admit that my decision to rent a newer place had not turned out well. For good or ill, I vowed I wouldn't do that again.

14

CALL OF THE WHITE ELEPHANT

Under "Houses for Rent," I saw a house in Wellesley, built in1924, which had been renovated in the late 1970s, that had potential. The small two-story house was two miles from the center of town, which was close enough to walk to. The town itself boasted Wellesley College, Babson College, Massachusetts Bay Community College, and Dana Hall School. It had a symphony, several libraries, and, best of all, the Boston Marathon ran through it on Route 135, across from Wellesley College, on Patriots Day, the third week of April each year.

Oh, how I wanted to run in the marathon. I ran every day, averaging forty miles a week, to stay in shape and because I enjoyed it. But leaving Faust at home in order to run nettled him even though we had bicycled together that morning. As I changed into my running clothes, he would sit with his back against the kitchen door, with imagined crossed forearms, asking me, "How dare you not take me?"

Plainly he couldn't run with me with paws on the ground doing six or seven miles a day. Even if he could have done the distance and had been fast enough to keep up with me, his lung problem would have prevented it. Alternatively, he wouldn't have been able to endure jouncing on my sweaty shoulders as I jogged and ran. Sorry, kiddo.

However, in spite of my faithful running schedule, I knew the marathon was never to be in my future. My chipped right kneecap was becoming increasingly less tolerant of the concussive forces from running, irrespective of the surface I ran on or the padding and configuration of my running shoes. While I could tolerate seven miles a day, the possibility of my achieving over twenty-six miles of continuous running footfalls in one day was, sadly, becoming laughable. That was all the more reason to enjoy running the marathon vicariously, screaming, clapping, and cheering on all the runners before jogging home to see the winners on TV as they approached the finish line on Boylston near the Boston Public Library.

Wellesley was a bedroom community fifteen miles west of Boston and known as "Tree City USA." This was not only for its many tree-studded streets and properties but also for its cultivation of horticulture. There was the Massachusetts Horticultural Society located at the Elm Bank Horticultural Center, the gardens around the town hall, and those at Wellesley College's Botanic Gardens and the H.H. Hunnewell Arboretum.

As soon as I could, I arranged for the listing realtor to show Faust and me the house and give us a brief guided tour of Wellesley. It was a rental with an option to buy. As much as I would have loved to own a house, I didn't see that happening financially any time in the near future. When I called Harriet, the realtor, I mentioned that I'd have Faust with me. While she hesitated a second, probably wondering why on earth I'd have an animal with me, she replied that would be fine. Well, I suspected it wasn't going to be *all that fine.*

When I met her at her office, she did a double-take. Apparently she assumed I would have Faust enclosed and not on my shoulders as he usually traveled. I wasn't trying to be sneaky not explicitly stating how he traveled. It simply had never occurred to me to mention his neck-draping habit.

"Oh, I ... I thought you meant ... I mean, I thought your cat would be in a travel carrier. This is highly unusual. Although, well ... uh ... maybe not a problem." Faust just looked at her casually as she stumbled on, "I mean ... I don't have anything against cats ... but ... well, if I get cat hair in the car and any other clients are allergic to cats ..."

"We could take my car if you'd prefer. I vacuumed it recently, and Faust doesn't sit on the passenger seat so there should be very little, if any, cat hair there. Is that okay with you?"

"Well, I guess that would be all right. Okay, sure," she agreed although she didn't seem all that sanguine about the arrangement. After pretending not to carefully inspect the passenger seat for lurking globs of clingy gray fur, she somewhat unwillingly seated herself, leaning away from the seatback and pressing her feet hard to the floor as if to levitate above the seat cushion.

From the look on her face, she would have given almost anything to have had a clean bath towel to sit on. She seemed sure she would inadvertently transfer this cat's detritus into her car. That meant she would have to have the car's interior cleaned before escorting another client in it. As if feeling insulted by her negative body language, Faust hopped from my shoulders into my lap, letting loose hair and dander fly around. With a chuckle Jim Croce's lyrics came to mind, "And you don't mess around with ... Faust." Harriet emitted a soft grunt of disapproval.

Shortly we arrived at a dusty-pink house with black shutters which rose fifteen feet above the street level. Underneath it was a deep single-car garage.   As I started to pull into the narrow, concrete-walled driveway, I saw there were no steps in the walls leading directly from the asphalt driveway to the house so I reversed and parked on the street. In front of me now were two concrete steps leading to the large-slab concrete front walkway. The concrete was old, cracked, and chipped. I wondered why someone over the years had not installed blue stone pavers instead or at least repaired or replaced the decrepit concrete.

Harriet led us to the elevated front door area which rested likewise on four feet of old, unobscured concrete. As she ascended the wrought-iron-railing-sided front steps, Faust focused on a magnolia tree which stood there to our right by the walkway. Sniffing, he was attempting to capture the strong, sweet scent of the recent blooms. He had never smelled one before, even when we made our pilgrimages to Lexington Gardens nursery. Faust's last olfactory exploration there, however, nearly resulted in our expulsion as he tried to gastronomically determine which potted catnip plant had the most piquant flavor.

The magnolia flowers were three-and one-inch diameter cups of deep pink at the base with white, strap-shaped petals. These blossoms were quite magnificent to behold until they died. As was obvious here, when they dropped, they lay rotting like so much garbage beneath the large, leathery-leafed tree. While these deep-green, glossy leaves were dramatic, they too apparently tended to continually drop into the vile-smelling area below. I had heard that grass did not to grow under a magnolia. Perhaps that was why this tree had its roots embedded in a large circular area that was blanketed with pine bark mulch.

As I leaned closer to the tree, I noticed there was some black material that looked like carbon black on the bark. On closer inspection it appeared to be sooty mold. It may have been the symptom of some pest infestation, part of the tree's aging process, or possibly both. Whatever it was, I didn't want Faust scratching his claws on the bark or trying to climb the tree. The idea of his getting the spores on his paws and fur and then spreading the mold on me as well as around in the house was revolting. Furthermore, my having to clean up after that tree didn't register on my Thrill-O-Meter.

It reminded me of when I was a child in rural Pennsylvania. We had a huge catalpa tree in the front yard with its large heart-shaped leaves and equally-large white orchid-like flowers. When the flowers died, they fluttered to the grass, creating a soggy, smelly mess that dried into papier mâché, making it very difficult to rake up. Even worse were the long, dark-brown pods which dropped to the ground in late summer. As they fell, they opened, dispersing hundreds of two-winged flat seeds which slowly helicoptered to the ground. Raking the hard, wooden shells was nearly impossible, ultimately requiring me to pick them up one at a time by hand when I had yard duty. Suddenly back in the present, I physically jerked away from the magnolia. Even though Faust was nowhere near the bark, it struck me as the safer thing to do.

A grass lawn continued to climb toward the two-tier backyard. Large maples stood stalwartly along the irregular property line. A bare rock ledge to which an old mountain ash tree clung tenaciously with its tangle of bare roots sat on the right hand side at the beginning of the second tier. It was near a seventy-two-inch tall, Western Red Cedar picket fence which had been left to weather gracefully. In front of the ledge was an ancient apple tree, still struggling to produce fruit while being lovingly attended by a mass of bees.

Faust was surveying the property, becoming interested in getting down. The tightening muscles of his back legs in preparation for his jumping showed his enthusiasm. He knew this could be a great place for him to play with his Wiffle Ball or chase after his clothesline. He could scale the crooked apple tree and survey his kingdom from its gnarled upper branches. He could pretend to chase birds and squirrels. If he found any grasshoppers, he could practice his feline attack behaviors which were by now pretty well non-existent or rudimentary at best. I wondered if I'd be responsible for mowing the massive area or if the owner would have someone come in to tend to it.

Harriet had unfastened the lock box and unlocked the front door. "Are you ready?" she asked.

Immediately past the hollow-core front door which needed resurfacing was a small, sunny room in eggshell white with windows on two sides. One was looking over the magnolia and three were looking over the street. The original wood floor glowed with a hand-hewed vibe of natural warmth that had seen a lot of life. Frequently homes had carpet everywhere—and I do mean "everywhere." I'd even seen it in bathrooms. That totally boggled my mind. Where was the user consultancy when this was being planned? How could a builder, or even a homeowner, not see the possibility of shower moisture nourishing mold underneath the weave? And what about those pesky droplets of liquid that missed going into the toilet bowl? Or the total regurgitation of toilet contents when there was a clog? That was too disgusting.

Because this was the sunny side of the house, the first room would be a great place to grow houseplants on the window sills. Under the front-facing windows, was an old-fashioned radiator designed to be the primary provider of heat for the room. Painted white and not yet chipping or flaking, it looked better than in its original factory dull aluminum. But it really needed a radiator cover to make it a touch more post-industrial as well as more useful for a cat desiring to soak up some rays.

As Harriet talked about the room, I wondered if I could use this as my office where I could write and coach clients. While its close proximity to the front door made it good for clients, it was less acceptable as a location for what my office required. There was no door to close to set it off from the rest of the house. The coat closet could potentially accommodate a three-drawer file cabinet, paper supplies, and printer. But there was no reasonable space for my desk, fax-copier, phone, and computer, which I had yet to acquire, if I had client seating. To put everything in this one room would feel claustrophobic. But if I met with clients in the sun room and had my actual office upstairs, it would mean running up and down stairs to make copies of contracts, coaching exercises, reference materials, and anything else I deemed useful. That would be clumsy and unprofessional.

Unfortunately, the room was probably better as a reading and plant room, a place where Faust and I could sit and meditate amongst greenery. In the autumn we could watch the local hardwoods' colorful leaves swirl in the brisk seasonal winds. Then in the winter we could marvel as the snow fell delicately outside, blanketing the yard, creating grotesque and ethereal figures out of the shrubs and trees.

At that moment Faust began acting strangely. He was fidgeting, wiggling to get down. He usually stayed put around my shoulders, acting nonchalant, disinterested in the inconsequential activities of other humans. But something had his attention. I put him down. He began sniffing. It was as if he had latched onto some particularly magnetic scent and was desperate to explore every inch of the floor, corners, baseboard, under the radiator, and front and closet doors to find its source.

"Are *you* ready to see the living room?" Harriet asked as I was seemingly less attentive than she wanted me to be. I followed along as she talked about how the sun room flowed into a narrow living room. "Because the living room is rectangular instead of square, you can be closer to the fireplace, but not so close as to be uncomfortable. Moreover, with three front windows opposite the old-red brick fireplace and one on the other side of the building you have lots of natural light." From here I could see that wood floors prevailed downstairs except for linoleum in the kitchen which I spied through the opening to the right of the fireplace.

The fireplace brick hearth, in need of appointing, drew Faust immediately to it. Even though ashes still coated the fire box, Faust sprinted inside and immediately gazed up into the chimney. I couldn't tell if he had heard a bird or squirrel lurking about on the roof or something nesting precariously inside the chimney. Stretching against the brick wall, he tried hoisting a leg to gain purchase to climb up.

Harriet gasped, dramatically clutching her breast. "Oh, my god! Get him out of there. He's creating a mess! He's going to track ashes throughout this sparklingly clean house. He should not have come with us."

Without a word, but with a pained expression, I carefully removed his paws which were now light gray. "Excuse me a moment while I take care of this." Embarrassed, I quickly took Faust outside to rub his paws, harness, and leash clean on the grass and dust off my now-light-gray-foot-printed blouse. "For heaven's sake, Faust, what's going on with you? This isn't like you. If you don't behave, I'll put you … uh … in the car."

Of course, he knew that was a bluff. I would never do that because it would be too hot too quickly in the car, even with all the windows cranked down several inches. No, he knew I'd always take him with me. Even on cold, cloudy days where I'd be gone for five minutes max, I invariably took him into stores or public buildings. Some patrons and staff undoubtedly thought I was crazy but I had no intention of taking a chance with him. When there wasn't the risk of hyperthermia, there was the risk of his crawling under the seat and getting his harness caught on the position-change mechanism and strangling himself.

Back in the living room again, this time looking out the front-facing windows, I could see heavy hooks above the windows on the outside. It looked as though old-fashioned, heavy wood storm windows would be hung there for the fall and winter. As Harriet talked again about the benefits of this house as a rental and as a purchase, she asked, "Have you considered buying? We haven't already talked about this but this could be a great deal for you. All your rent would apply to the purchase price."

I didn't respond right away because I was concentrating on the windows. The windows themselves were old, double-hung, with single-pane glass needing putty replacement in different corners. I wondered about significant heat loss in cold weather. Making it worse was the fact that the room's radiators were positioned under these windows, allowing heat to readily escape through the thin glass. The windows would require blinds and curtains. Moreover, rising just below the windows outside was a tall, wide, dense juniper foundation planting which made access to the windows for hanging and securing the storm windows problematic.

Still pursuing my possibly buying, Harriet continued, "The comps on this house are quite good. Being on a quiet, tree-lined street, with a large grassed yard, and great curb-appeal, it is a real bargain." As I caught her drift, I smiled as if I were taking it under advisement.

To the right, through a large squared-off arch, was a long dining room with white chair rails and a build-in white dish cabinet which Harriet said she thought were "lovely touches." Faust made the mistake of placing his paws on the round drawer knobs on the dish cabinet to try to look through the glass-paned doors above. Even elongated to his full-length, he wasn't quite tall enough to see into its empty shelves.

When Harriet turned to point out its carpentry, she saw him. About to gasp again, she demanded, "Don't do that! Do *not* touch the cabinet. You might scratch it." He didn't respond to her. I could hear her breathing more deeply. As her face reddened, a blood vein protruded on her neck, pulsing.

My attention refocused to the dish cabinet, I immediately thought, "While I understand your concern, Harriet, he isn't using his claws. But, okay." As I signaled him with a soft "Down," he sat. Then I crooked my index finger toward me and he walked to my side. Anyone carefully observing his behavior likely would have made the canine comparison and thought "How very like Lassie-like he is."

Faust would have found such thoughts insulting. Even, philosophically, on Homer's "Golden Chain" that was supposed to reach down from Heaven to Earth, cats were surely several links above such insignificant, groveling creatures as dogs. However, from the currently satisfied look on his white-whiskered face, I knew he had already done all he wanted to do before Harriet had issued her commands. From the look on his face he was likely thinking, "Jeez, lady, chill out. Don't sweat the small change."

In the center of the plastered ceiling was a fourteen-by-fourteen-inch square, flat, heavy, mirrored lighting fixture which was jammed with sixteen clear bulbs. When turned on full, it was like a stage klieg light which created temporary blindness. Definitely overkill. Its size and obvious weight felt gravitationally intimidating, seeming on the verge of crashing down. Clearly it could function quite well with only a third the bulbs and look, and feel, even better.

This light's intended design reminded me of architect Walter Gropius' 1938 modernist home which I had visited. Located on five and a half acres at 68 Baker Bridge Road, in Lincoln, MA, the Bauhaus-like building had started out as a showcase and an example of modernist landscape architecture in America for students at Harvard University Graduate School of Design where Gropius taught. It was the epitome of simplicity, uncluttered, non-traditional lines, and efficiency. But despite its use of modern technology and line, it was a warm and inviting home. This modern ceiling fixture was anything but simple, clean, and uncluttered.

The dining room walls above the chair rails had

been papered in natural, flat-woven grass cloth in warm native hues which Harriet discussed at length, addressing its "elegance" and the expenditure involved in using it for the entire room. While the texture was appealing, the color looked out of place with the chair rails and built-in. Perhaps if painted a pale Nantucket blue-gray, the grass cloth would have looked more fitting to the attempted semi-formality of the room. Even though the wall covering looked as though it had been designed to lure the raking of cat nails, Faust didn't show any interest in it. Always a gentleman cat, he would have thought it crude and impolite to ravage anyone's walls to sharpen his talons.

In spite of its having three windows, the room was dark. This lack of natural light surprised me. One window looked out over the concrete entrance to the house and the magnolia, still dropping its flowers and leaves. Two other windows brought the shadowed green serenity of the backyard indoors. While that view was soothing, without sunshine penetrating to illuminate the room, the dining area was somewhat depressing, always requiring artificial light.

"Next is a very light, open kitchen which has lots of countertops and up and down cabinets." Through a white swinging door, we followed Harriet into a long kitchen in eggshell with aqua Formica counters that were chipped at their previously sharp corners. Placement of appliances was less than optimal.

On the left wall, behind the fireplace, was the gas stove. Faust raced toward it, slunk down, and stuck his forearm under it, excitedly reaching for something. Hopefully it was a dust bunny but I suspected it was something with multiple legs and a hard shell. Harriet furrowed her brow then pretended not to notice. Her body tension spoke volumes. As she pointed out the refrigerator, Faust raced over to it, again hunkered down, with his head on the floor, facing underneath, intent upon another something. I waited for her to show her displeasure but she only inhaled deeply again. Her action didn't look like a prayerful exercise.

Evidently, this was not how things were supposed to be done in her world. Consequently, she was aggrieved and just barely disguising it. If Faust annoyed her, I wondered how she handled screaming children, uncontrolled by their client parents, rampaging around the house and property she was attempting to show, something I had seen at Open Houses. Unbeknownst to her, this was not how things were done in Faust's world either ... at least under normal circumstances.

The refrigerator was stowed to the stove's left in a cubbyhole between the door from the dining room and a opening back into the living room. Opening the right-hinged refrigerator door blocked the living room entrance. Ironically, if it had been left-hinged, there would have been no way to access its contents, unless you did it from the living room.

However, what I was particularly discomforted

by was the swinging door from the dining room. It could easily catch and squish a certain cat following his human companion from one room to the next unless I used a rubber doorstop to hold it open all the time ... and hoped it wouldn't somehow become dislodged by human accident or cat play. To be safe I'd have to take it off its hinges but then there would be nothing to block the view of kitchen activity from guests or hinder cooking smells from drifting into the dining room. But given how infrequently we had guests after Alix, I suspect it wouldn't really matter all that much.

Faust left the refrigerator to settle by the stove, out of harm's way, as if to patiently wait for me to finish. Then he lowered his head and extended his neck as he focused on the floor where the beige linoleum met the cabinets' toe kick along the outer wall. What did he have his eye on? I wondered. Please don't let it be cockroaches. As it turned out, if I had looked closely, I would have known ... what I really did not want to know.

A large window above an old, but well-maintained, porcelain sink looked out onto the tranquil backyard with its two concrete steps leading onto the second grassy tier. Because the space between the sink and the stove was too wide, well over five feet and ungainly, Harriet suggested, "You could put in an island to make food preparation even easier."

As I eyeballed the space, I smiled. She was probably talking off the top of her head and hadn't actually measured it. An island would have been a serious impediment to movement if there had actually been enough room for any size island not on casters. Besides, there was no place to store it when not in use. What the kitchen really needed for some food preparation convenience was a four-foot floor cabinet with a countertop to the right of the stove and a small countertop to the left of the stove to receive foodstuffs taken from the refrigerator. Currently there was a tiny Formica-covered shelf to the left of the stove but it was only large enough to hold a telephone. One thing you could say about the kitchen was that it undoubtedly had not been designed by a woman.

Intruding low into the room at the far end was the diagonal stairwell wall. This significantly limited the area where one could place a small dinette bistro table and two chairs. It looked like a breakfast nook accessible only by little people. Furthermore, once you located the essential cabinet with countertop to the right of the stove, the "eat-in" area no longer existed. That left a dark, cramped corner, not even tall enough for an accessible trash receptacle. It was less than serviceable even for Faust's dishes.

At the end, off to the right, there was an oddly-designed addition. Harriet raved about it, saying, "This handy addition provides a floor-to-ceiling pantry for storage. And even better, a bathroom on the first floor."

Suddenly Faust skittered across the floor into a

room on the far wall. Now what? Was he chasing something ... or just having a little fun? The room was a super-compact, aqua-tiled half-bath with a window overlooking the side yard, with its low stone wall and rocky outcropping, and bi-fold door which faced the door to the stairs down to the basement. Faust was hunkered down in the small space behind the toilet.

You've heard the unkind, feline-derisive expression about "not enough room to swing a cat," (sorry, Faust). Well, in this bathroom space you would be fortunate to be able to simply turn around if you had any excess weight. While you sat on the toilet, the sink on the left was nearly in your lap. Furthermore, the bi-fold door missed scraping the sink by mere inches as you opened it. In emergencies when you couldn't make it upstairs, it would have been a godsend ... as long as you did not pinch your fingers in the bi-fold as you closed it quickly and not smash your hip on the sink before you reached your destination.

It reminded me of a bathroom in an owner-built house I had inspected years before, one that appeared to have been conceived during an LSD trip. It was seven-feet-long, perhaps five-feet wide from wall to wall, with a tiny sink on the right between jutting cabinets and drawers which reached from the door all the way past the toilet at the end of the room. No cabinets or drawers could be opened more than an inch when you reached the toilet space. And nothing within reach was at all useable when you were ensconced there.

Having finished in the bathroom, Faust was now rubbing his paws against the closed basement door, showing he wanted to inspect the lower level … now. As I exited the half-bath, I recognized that the basement door would have to be closed *all the time* because anyone leaving the bathroom could easily plunge into the waiting abyss if it weren't.

"Paws down, Faust," I quietly commanded. "You can inspect the basement when we do. That will be soon." As if acceding to my wishes, he sat by the door, unmoving, despite eagerness exuding from every kitty pore. His tail tapped the floor. Then he leaned around to paw it one more time as if to challenge my dictate. At which point I picked him up to remind him I was the alpha in our relationship. Of course, as he raised his whiskers and looked askance at me, I knew he knew better.

To the right of the half-bath was a four-foot-by-four-foot space, where two doors were placed at ninety-degrees to one another. The first was to the pantry requiring a step ladder for the two upper shelves and the second was to the backyard. Open one and you block the other. Faust's attention was drawn to the pantry and he tried to extricate himself from my grip without success to explore it.

For a quick inspection of the property, we stepped outside this one-story architect's add-on nightmare. When I glanced back at it, it looked like a wart on the house's right buttock. As we strolled in the grass around the house, with Harriet pointing out positive attributes, I let Faust down.

He ran and rolled around at the end of his lead, reveling. Along the deeply-shadowed back fence between the towering trees were draping blue-flowered vinca and fragrant yellow azaleas in bloom. With so many trees and shrubs and so much beautiful green grass the yard was more inviting than the house. As we breathed in the clean air, Harriet touted the many restful uses , of the backyard.

15

TOO MANY VISITORS

Once again inside, Harriet listed the many benefits of the second floor room location as we headed for the main staircase, off the living room. Three steps up, the stairs made a quick dog-leg to the right. Because it was on the dark side of the house, the stairwell had a small window ten feet up the wall for additional light. Following Harriet, I proceeded to ascend the bare wood steps toward the efficiently-small full bathroom at the top on the left.

Faust was acting agitated. Suddenly, he exploded from my arms. The leash snapped out of my hand. He ran up the stairs. I thought I had heard something before he hurled himself upward. It sounded like scratching. Charging ahead, he passed Harriet just before she landed on the top step. I was right behind him. In the bathroom he hopped onto the toilet, which paralleled the back wall, and looked out the small window with great anticipation.

As soon as I caught hold of the bathroom door jamb and slipped myself inside, I saw what had attracted Faust's attention. A young raccoon was leaning from the eave outside the window attempting to reach the wide window ledge. When we were outside, I hadn't looked at the roof. Of course, I should have to see the condition of the roof, gutters, and chimney. If only I had ... Maybe that was what Faust had heard inside the chimney earlier. On the ground below, where we had been only minutes before, I could see a mama raccoon with two other babies, looking up, pacing back and forth. Maternal concern covered her furry, masked face.

Faust was tapping on the window pane. "Stop it, Faust!" I whispered, afraid the little critter outside was going to try to respond or try to land on the exterior sill and lose its balance. Just then another small paw reached down. Oh, no! There were two young raccoons on the roof. How did they get there? What could I, should I, do? Rescue scenarios threaded through my brain like old celluloid film on the sprockets of a thirty-five-millimeter projector. Opening the window was not a solution.

Scanning the roof edge from the bathroom to the one-story kitchen addition to my left, I saw a large, low maple branch just a foot above it. That must have been how they accessed the roof in the first place. Great! I quietly picked Faust up so the babies would no longer be distracted. They could continue to work their way over the roof to the addition to the branch, scoot along it, and then climb down the fifty-foot-tall maple tree's trunk at the top of the steps to the yard's upper level. I wondered what that said about the true usability of the fireplace ... or about the likelihood of furry critters entering the house uninvited.

Next on the left wall was an adequate linen closet followed by three small bedrooms off the narrow hall. One room faced the backyard and two faced the front. Each bedroom had wood floors and a four-foot wide by two-foot deep closet that was typical of the1920s construction. I'd have to add area rugs to keep my feet warm in winter and an armoire or clothing rack to handle my small wardrobe. Spreading clothing out among three closets wasn't appealing. In the ceiling at the end of the hallway was the covered square cut-out access to the attic. It didn't look to have a pull-down staircase. Faust would have been delighted to check it out if it had. Of course, he had already mastered ladders: so much for easy, unaccompanied attic inspection.

Harriet was talking about the radiators, "Each room has a radiator. The heat flows well from them on the second floor. They're practical and look in good shape." Of course, they too needed radiator covers. Then she added, "And there's also a cedar-lined closet for storing winter woolies in addition to the regular clothes closet in the second front bedroom." Each bedroom had three windows providing varying amounts of illumination but no overhead lights in the eight-foot high ceilings. That was inconvenient.

By the time we were back downstairs in the kitchen to check out the basement, Faust was sniffing again, eager to do some discovering. The stairs descending into the basement were long and steep. Rather than let Faust dangerously squirm in anticipation in my arms, I put him down where upon he immediately bolted, dashing off into the dark unknown. As Harriet flipped on the light switch at the top of the stairs, I grasped the railing on the left hand side and started down. Maybe, over time, I'd get used to feeling I was being pulled forward into the void, like Caitlin in my novel.

The large area was broken up by the chimney in the center of the room, with a white-painted, floor-to-ceiling, six-foot-wide built-in bookcase on the front of the brick surface and the furnace and hot water heater on the rear. A laundry sink was against the back wall beside the washer and dryer. Harriet was pleased to announce, "They come with the rental and can go with the purchase price."

To the right and forward of the bookcase was an awkwardly-located red steel column, a telescoping, adjustable jack post to support the sagging floor joists of the living room above. It would interfere with moving large objects in and out of the room by way of the garage. As I looked up at the un-plastered ceiling, I didn't see any batt or blanket insulation between the joists. I followed the naked joists all the way to the back of the house. That likewise was going to contribute to a heating problem.

Constructed to the right of and perpendicular to the washer and dryer was a five-foot-long, wood work table, with two shelves below and a large tool pegboard above, on the wall shared with the garage. Faust was now running full-tilt around the red-painted floor, his leash flapping behind him, in pursuit of something. He disappeared. Then he bounded from the blackness under the stairs to sprint under the work table. I could hear a scuffle. I froze for a moment. What manner of creature had somehow found entrance into basement? Surely not a raccoon. Hopefully not a snake.

As Faust crawled out, I mentally gulped. Languishing in his mouth was a small gray mouse, its pointed snout and round ears twitching and black button eyes glistening. As Faust looked up at me to proudly show me his prize, the drool-coated mouse wrenched itself free and skittered away to hide under the water heater. Oh, crap! Not mice!

Harriet, upon seeing the little rodent drop from Faust's mouth, blanched. Then after a pregnant pause, she calmly excused the singular rodent by suggesting it had probably come in when someone recently tested the garage door. "Don't worry. A few mouse traps here would do the trick and then it could be disposed of easily. No problem."

Sure, no problem. I picked Faust up again, gingerly dusting the cobwebs off his fur, keeping away from his mouse-tainted mouth, and headed toward the door to the garage. The fire-rated, insulated, metal door, which opened into the basement, revealed a long, narrow, white-painted, cold concrete room. Running the length of the house, it was a single-car garage which was able to accommodate two compact cars end to end. This was where the storm windows were stored. The garage door was manual and boasted a heavy-duty spring, making it easy to open and close it. As I was looking up at the spring, my focus shifted to the ceiling. Even though this area was under the sun room and dining room, there was no insulation between the joists here either. I rolled my eyes. This was another circumstance that didn't bode well for heat maintenance on the first floor and in general.

Even though we had spent only thirty minutes doing the walk-through, it had felt like hours. My enthusiasm had started to dwindle after Faust had pursued hearing something in the chimney. I wondered what else besides raccoons and mice was lurking. So many little things about this rental had added to my disappointment.

While I loved the idea of having a yard, trees, and possible garden area, there was a lot to take care of. Where could I work with clients? The kitchen was awkward and inefficient. There were rooms I'd never use that had to be heated and cooled. There was no air-conditioner either. While Faust would have been delighted with any number and type of wild animal traversing the roof and getting into the chimney, I wasn't interested in making the fireplace off-limits for additional heating which I suspected would likely be needed.

As for the prospect of having to try to locate and remove *the* mouse, I knew there was undoubtedly a multitude of its twitchy, little, fast-breeding friends and family, as well as their nests and droppings. I'd want them O-U-T. And not just out of the basement. Faust had repeatedly indicated by his actions on the first floor that his scaly-tailed friends were not confined to the basement. And who knew how they were getting into the house. Was it really *just* the garage?

It was a given that with the single-pane windows, questionable use of the fireplace, unused rooms, and lack of installation of any Owings Corning Pink batts in the basement and garage ceilings the winter heating bills were likely to be gigantic. And I hadn't even investigated the attic space to see what insulation was likely missing there. Except for its availability, this house had many more *cons* than *pros*.

Back in the car, Harriet who now appeared resigned to no-sale, rental or otherwise, asked with a constructed smile, "So tell me how you feel about the house? How does it fit your needs? Do you think it could work for you?"

"My first impression is that while it's a nice house, it is more house than I want. I think I need something smaller."

Faust was again around my neck. But seemingly either bored or unhappy about the negative atmosphere, he repositioned his body so his head was to my left. That left his tail to flick in Harriet's direction, a gesture that was not lost on her. I took my right hand off the key in the ignition to tap him on his butt. He stopped. That was okay. He had already made his point.

"What about an apartment?" she asked, looking as if she'd prefer not to go through this house routine again.

"I need the quiet and privacy of a house so I can see clients."

A look darted instantaneously across her face as if she were once again entreating God to give her strength. Why was He punishing her? Hadn't she already put up a lot with this strange cat-obsessed person and her poorly-controlled animal which clearly had queered this deal? "Why not rent an apartment in which to live and an office in which to see clients?"

Paying for an office as well as a place to live was out of the question. I asked, "Do you have any houses for rent that are smaller than fifteen hundred square feet of living space? And maybe a little newer? I don't need a basement or large yard but I do need a garage, especially in the winter."

"Not currently. But I can let you know if something comes on the market."

I said, "Fine. Thanks. I'd appreciate it." But I didn't expect to hear from Harriet again which was probably just as well. Faust's presence seemed to chafe her and I wasn't going to house-hunt without him. However, as per her agreement, she then directed me through town, pointing out places of interest. After twenty minutes, I dropped her off at her office and headed back to Sudbury.

16

GUEST HOUSE WITH "BENEFITS?"

As I continued to peruse the paper's rental market ads, Faust became increasingly displeased by my misdirected attention. He'd hop onto my lap at my desk and work his way under the flattened sheets of newsprint where I was attempting to circle possible rentals. As if playing, he'd slither out the other side, hook my pen with a paw, and slap the newspaper, occasionally slashing it with a claw. Then he'd look at me as if demanding me to hurry up and play with him. After all, he needed to remind me that I had obligations to fulfill.

One ad finally caught my eye. It was for a guest cottage in south Wayland, just off Route 27. The realtor's name was Claudia Smissman, Alix's neighbor in Wayland. Claudia was a tall, blonde, comely Nordic-type, and seemed to be a no-nonsense person. The few times I had seen her I pictured her in contradictory ways: on a fashion runway, strutting her stuff for Yves Saint Laurent, or sprinting to the finish in women's 100 meters for the Olympics.

I called her office to ask about the rental. Unfortunately, it had already been seized. She suggested I come in to her office to check out what was still available. I boogied on down with Faust on my shoulders. With my work, scrubbing areas of the house of cat allergens that I could now close off, and looking for a place to live, I had been pre-occupied and less available to him for which I felt guilty. Maybe this little trip would make amends to some degree.

At Claudia's office on Route 20, several people were on the phone, talking with buyers, sellers, and those offering and inquiring about rental properties. I was glad they were busy because it suggested there was a market out there from which to choose. But, simultaneously, I was discouraged that it likewise meant the competition for any individual rental was likely to be stiff.

Claudia, who was dressed in a low-cut blouse and short skirt, greeted me and Faust with a warm smile and seated us at her paper-cluttered steel desk. As I explained that I was more interested in a small house than in an apartment, Claudia slowly thumbed through a large white ring binder which had detail sheets of rentals in clear plastic envelopes. With each rental she shared a brief anecdote about the property and owner.

We were about ten pages into the small-house rental listings when she stopped and started to laugh. At that point Faust shifted to my lap. I thought the house looked good from its photo and the specs made it sound ideal. It was a one bedroom, one bath, furnished house, single story, just under 1,000 square feet, renovated the year before, with a washer, dryer, dishwasher, and air-conditioner on less than an eighth of an acre, with a tiny garage, small lawn, flower beds, and place for a veggie garden. So what did she find so funny?

When Claudia stopped laughing, she apologized. "I'm sorry about that. That listing should have been removed. This place would have been ideal for you, but, you know, it had big problems." I wondered if they had discovered termites or mold.

Shaking her head, she explained, "A month ago I received a call here at the office from an individual who said he was considering renting his house. You know, he described the house location, its features, and all the upgrades he had made. Then he asked if I'd come see it. He said he had seen my card and, you know, had heard good things about how I handled clients. He didn't give me the name of his referral. I told him I couldn't leave right then but, you know, would have my assistant take a quick look that afternoon. My assistant came back with a photo and particulars. He said he was really impressed and, you know, that I should see it soon. So I set up an appointment with the owner for two days later.

"The owner was fortyish and attractive. I mean, he was nicely dressed and seemed very pleasant. The house was terrific, you know, in every detail. The asking rent was acceptable. But then things got a little strange. As we finished going over the house and grounds, he started making moves on me. I mean, I've had men come on to me before but this was different. You know, there was nothing flirtatious or subtle about it. He stated outright he wanted to have sex with me right then on the sofa. I mean, what a moron!

"I looked him in the eye and said, 'I'm sure you're a real tiger but do you want to list this house or not?' I mean, I hoped he was just fooling around. You know, making rude macho suggestions to see how I'd respond. Some men think that being sexually crude with a woman puts her in her place. You know, they think it's funny. I waited until he realized that it was real estate business or nothing."

"Had you ever had this kind of in-your-face problem with a potential client alone in his house before?"

"No. Being alone with a man doesn't bother me. I can usually handle myself in any situation. But this ..., you know, I wasn't so sure if he was just being a jerk or was someone who was planning to assault me. I thought if he'd back off and chill out, we could take on the listing."

"That kind of behavior would make me not want to be around him," I said.

"Generally, I can put this kind of guy in his place with a, you know, "give-me-a-break" look or a few well-chosen words. I mean, if he knocked it off and acted more business-like, I'd just sign him up. I could continue to work with him if he'd stop being a jackass. He said, you know, that because I was so 'attractive and seductive' he'd come on too strong and too brash. He apologized profusely. I acknowledged his apology. I mean, it seemed we were past all that nonsense. So we talked about the house for a few more minutes then we went over the contract details.

"But as I was putting the signed contract back into my briefcase, you know, he offered to 'dance' for me. Huh? I said, 'No thank you.' He walked over to me and began, you know, gyrating his hips real close to mine."

With my jaw at half-mast, I interjected, "Are you kidding? How disgusting! That's even more frightening! What did you do next? I hope you ran like hell out of there." Faust quietly shifted from my lap to my shoulders. He looked at Claudia, head cocked to the right side, seemingly intrigued by what she was saying.

"You know, I'd had my fill of this wacko. Before I could grab my handbag and briefcase from the coffee table, he unzipped his pants. I mean, he pulled out Mister Smiley and began slapping and rubbing him. I started for the exit. You know, I couldn't get out of the house fast enough. But at the front door he tapped me on the shoulder. I turned around. He extended his hand to me. You know, it was filled with 'Smiley juice'."

"Oh, that makes me want to gag! But you took his listing anyway?" I was astounded the office would take on someone who exhibited such potentially dangerous behavior. I couldn't imagine any woman having that pervert for a landlord, someone who probably still had keys to the house.

"Heavens, no!" she replied, pulling the detail sheet out of the plastic envelope and crumpling it. "My assistant must have already created the sheet for me, you know, and placed it in the listing book. I hadn't noticed it before or I would have removed it."

She hadn't seen it before today? My thoughts were spinning. She'd taken the listing a month ago! What if some other realtor had seen the listing and hadn't heard the story? What if that realtor had acted on the listing with a female client? What if I had been that client? Didn't they share those negative experiences among their colleagues? I began to wonder if there were any other rentals with detail sheets that needed to be pulled.

As if reading my mind, Claudia quickly added, "Don't worry. You know, this guy was an aberration. I mean, it never happened before or since." She laughed, but my heart had already sunk. Suddenly I couldn't wait to get away from Claudia's office's rental listings. As it turned out after we had gone through all the listings, the only one that was even remotely close to what I wanted was the one for the pervert's house.

It now occurred to me that you might never know anything about the person who owned the home you were renting, if he or she had tendencies for untoward behavior. Likewise, you might never know when the person renting you a house might just show up, allegedly wanting to check things, even when you weren't home. And if it were someone like Claudia's client who dabbled in "penile choreography" or some other personality- or mental instability, how would you know ahead of time? People who rent out their houses don't have to take a Rorschach test or the Minnesota Multiphasic Personality Inventory to assess their hidden "proclivities." None of this had ever crossed my mind before.

Claudia said she would keep in touch. I didn't blame her for what happened. It wasn't her fault. But I blamed her for my now knowing that such things could happen, not only to realtors but, perhaps, also to renters. It was like learning after the fact that the person who constructed your home was unlicensed, used inferior materials and off-the-street common laborers as plumbers and electricians. There had been something emotionally comforting about my former state of naiveté. Being smarter about things while necessary didn't always make me feel better.

We headed home with Faust standing on my lap, staring out my side window. A flock of robins flew overhead. With his paws on the side window, he tweeted and chattered at them, seemingly mimicking their sounds, vocalizations thought to be part of a cat's hunting technique. With Faust I'd never know if it would work. Because Faust had been on his best behavior at Claudia's I stopped at the grocery store, plopped him in his knapsack, and we bought a can of salmon for him.

17

THE "CON" IN CONFIDENCE

A week later around three-thirty in the afternoon
the doorbell rang. I was engrossed in writing an
article for the *Boston Business Journal* on Larry
Speakes and how the Boston-area public relations
community was responding to his tell-all book
about being press secretary to President Reagan.
Faust was curled upon my lap, napping. At the
sound he vaulted over the desk and made tracks for
the chair by the living room window, perhaps
somehow expecting to see Alix again. He pressed his
left paw on the glass. When I looked through the
door's peephole, I discovered a thirty-something
with tousled hair the color of spun sugar, impudent
blue eyes, honed cheek bones, an aquiline nose,
and a provocative smile in his squared jaw. He
reminded me of Robert Redford in *Out of Africa*.
Now that was a pleasant interruption, I thought,
and grinned.

From my restricted viewpoint I couldn't see a
clipboard or briefcase. Glancing back at Faust's
location, I opened the door slightly and twisted
myself through it onto the stoop. This contortion
was a safeguard whenever anyone came to the door.
Faust could be relied upon to personally check out

visitors. He especially loved meeting new people who would likely become his next reverential audience.

Tall, slim, and athletic-looking, the stranger was dressed in a button-down short-sleeve, light blue Oxford cloth shirt which enhanced his eyes and pressed khaki Dockers. He held something in his left hand. To my relief it looked like several pieces of mail instead of magazine subscription order forms or religious pamphlets desiring to "save" me.

I'd encountered that salvation mindset at Baylor University in Waco, Texas, where I was often referred to as a "heathen" because I was from Massachusetts, wore sneakers with stockings instead of black suede loafers with heavy white athletic socks, and wasn't a card-carrying Southern Baptist. The stranger was smiling engagingly at me. I smiled back, hopeful.

Immediately Faust started rapping his front paws double-time on the window. The expression on his face was difficult to read but he seemed desperate to communicate something. Was he miffed he couldn't meet the stranger? Or that it wasn't Alix? I couldn't decipher his code. I re-directed my attention to this good-looking guy at my door. Perhaps this was my reward for having been so productive today.

The stranger cocked his head to the right and fixed me with a hypnotic gaze as he spoke. "This Coldwater Creek catalogue came next door," he said, showing me one of the pieces of mail.

I did a mental double-take. It's not that I presumed this specimen of Hollywood eye candy would tell me he had lusted for me from afar and had finally galvanized the courage and girded his loins to meet me. But "This Coldwater Creek catalogue came next door" wasn't even in the running for the last thing I imagined him to say. Perplexed, I said, "I beg your pardon?" I didn't receive this catalogue so the post office hadn't mis-delivered it to him. I waited for the other shoe to drop.

With his costly dental investment gleaming at me again, he displayed one of those I-know-I'm-too-handsome-for-words-but-I-don't-want-to-make-a-big-deal-out-of-it looks. Granted he was unquestionably a stud muffin, and today he would have been a contender for *People Magazine*'s "Sexiest Man Alive" cover, but come on, fella, I was still waiting for an explanation. A minute or two slowly passed before he broke the spell, "My long-time girlfriend moved out last month," he said wistfully, "and I'm still receiving her catalogues."

I raised my eyebrows. Why was he here telling me this? Why didn't he simply chuck it in the circular file? My antennae began to vibrate. Biding my time to see what came next, I indicated, "Magazines and catalogues are not always forwarded by the post office."

Lowering his head, he glanced up through his eyebrows, giving him a charmingly boyish look, and said, "I thought, perhaps, you'd like to have it since it is apparel, accessories, and home décor for women."

Who was this guy? He said he lived next door but I'd never seen him before ... and I was sure I would have remembered if I had. Suddenly the possibility of a con game seeped into my thoughts. This scenario reminded me of a psychological compliance technique called "foot-in-the- door." It involves getting a person to agree to a modest request so the person would be more willing to later agree to a larger request. My accepting the offer of a catalogue could be considered agreeing to a "modest request."

As a result, I didn't want to agree to take the catalogue, just in case. At the same time I didn't want to seem uncivil by simply refusing it. As a child, I had been taught unequivocally that "good girls are *always* polite, no matter what." Once that sex-role stereotype had been embedded in my skull, it was hard to shake it loose even many decades later. He once again blinded me with his smile. Looking appropriately regretful, I said, "Thanks, that's thoughtful but I already receive it."

Deep down in the inner recesses of my brain I wanted it not to be a con. I wanted it to be that he was using this as a ploy—a rather clumsy ploy—to meet me because he sincerely wanted to get to know me. As I half-turned with my hand on the door handle to go in, I wondered if that would be the end of it.

Faust was slamming his paws hard against the

glass. Out of the corner of my eye I could see his ears were back as he pressed his face hard against the glass, flattening the left side of his head, making his eye bulge, raising his lip, and producing a fanged, maniacal expression. As I was opening the door a fraction of an inch, the other shoe dropped.

The stranger quickly said, pointing at Faust, "He seems upset. He's been tapping on the window since I arrived. Maybe," he said matter-of-factly, "he's trying hard to get your attention so he can meet me. I know I'd like to meet him."

Taken aback, I was scrambling to think of something to say when he continued, "He seems like quite a character. And those vampire fangs are great. I can see they're part of his charm. You must tell me about him. I'm sure he has an interesting story that I'd like to hear."

As he was finishing, I closed the door again. My unhinged, compressed-faced cat was still glaring at us. I still couldn't decide what to say. Maybe it wasn't a con. Maybe the stranger was just anxiously grasping at straws, trying too hard to make a good impression and keep the conversation going. I wasn't sure.

"I found Faust a number of years ago. He was hiding under my car in a parking lot. He is a lovely cat, talented, and very smart." As Faust persevered with his frenzied pummeling on the window, he resembled a character out of the movie, *Creepshow*.

"A rescue? Of course. I knew it," he said. I squinted at him, asking myself if he was for real.

202

Out of the blue he began waxing lyrical, "So that makes you an animal rescuer and devotee. That's so great! I'm impressed. I've never had animals but I can always spot an animal devotee. It's people like you who do the necessary hard work of rescuing and caring for homeless animals, and trying to get them adopted. And you accomplish wonderful things for them."

My brain was spinning as he babbled. I hadn't quite comprehended what was going on. When I started to respond, he persisted, "And I'll bet you know all about what draws and compels other animal devotees to donate and work for rescued animal shelters. I'll also bet you know how to reach those people and the public to get them to do all that."

I looked askance at him. The catalogue offer now clearly appeared to have been a pretense, concealing his real motives. But what was all this about rescuing animals? I pondered what he could possibly be after. As he paused, I said, "Yes, I have worked with rescue efforts."

"And that means you know all about how these homeless animal shelters work and what they need." He said it as if he knew this already. I began to speak when he rolled on, "That's so good of you to volunteer to help out rescued animals—giving of your time, effort, money, expertise, and experience. I mean it's such a charitable, caring, compassionate, and thoughtful thing to do. Thank God for volunteers like you. From what I've seen these animal shelters need all the help they can get. I'd very much like to hear about all the ways you've helped these shelters succeed financially."

I stood there overwhelmed by his ingratiating onslaught. Whoa! Wait a minute. What did he mean by my "helping animal shelters succeed financially"?

As if eavesdropping on my thoughts, he quickly switched his attention to Faust. "You said Faust— that *is* a great name by the way—is talented. I'd guess that means he does tricks. So what exactly does he do? You know, sit, stay, and shake? I would think a cat doing tricks is something out of the ordinary. That must mean you trained him. I can't imagine training a cat."

With so many assumptions and questions rushing at me, I cautiously said, "He dances on his hind legs and imitates all manner of 'dog' acrobatics."

"That's incredible. I would have thought cats were too aloof and independent to be trained."

As if by reflex, I suddenly wanted to correct him, to say that cats are very social and curious animals, and open to all sorts of new activities, like training. It's all in knowing how to stimulate their interest. But before I could say anything, he resumed his monologue.

"Training him must require a tremendous amount of time, effort, and patience. Now you've really tweaked my interest. I really want to see what you've trained him to do. I'm sure he'd like to give me a demonstration." He smiled a sort of come-hither smile and went on, "By his actions at the window I really think he's trying to get your attention so he can display his impressive repertoire for me. How about it? I'm sure Faust would love to show off for me."

All at once visions of Claudia's dancing-masturbator flickered before my eyes, further priming my barely submerged sense of apprehension. There was no question now. Something wasn't kosher here. No matter how handsome he was, there was no way I was inviting this manipulative stranger into my home. With a slight smile I said, "Perhaps some other time. Right now I'd better get back to work. Nice talking to you."

As I looked at him one last time, he held my gaze for a heartbeat longer than was socially necessary. Being an optimist about people, I emotionally still wanted his actions somehow to be sincere and innocent, in spite of their feeling bizarre and well-rehearsed slick.

As I began to slip through the partially open door again, he quickly spoke. I turned, wanting to shake my head and say, now what? He said, "Let me introduce myself. I'm Greg Rowen and I'm interested in animal shelters ... and *you*." On that note he pivoted and sauntered panther-like down across the lawn, mail still I hand. He disappeared from view on the other side of my garage.

I was flabbergasted. Throughout the

conversation he had been sending mixed messages. His body language clearly communicated he wanted me to know he was available and had unplumbed depths that I could explore. But his fast-talking approach and ham-handed, sycophantic speech made the interaction feel contrived and calculated. The encounter had left me convinced that despite his display of apparent ignorance about my past work with homeless animals, he already knew all about it. Moreover, that had been the real focus of the engagement.

Once the door closed behind me, Faust jumped off the chair and walked to me with deliberation, his ears back and tail slicing the air. He was breathing hard, his breaths whistling. "Calm down," I urged, stroking his back. "I don't want you to have an asthma attack." He wheezed and circled my ankles, rubbing against them. Teasing, I told him, "That was Greg Rowen who has an interest in you." He slapped my ankle. "Are you really sure you wouldn't like to do a little dance, just for him?" He slapped me again, harder. This time I felt his claws. No question. Faust was not amused by my question or its implication.

A few days later in the morning as I was walking Faust down Willow Road, Greg Rowen appeared in the next yard to my right almost from out of nowhere to call out hello. That took me totally by surprise. Doing so, he had interrupted Faust's promenade around the neighborhood which he loved. You could tell Faust enjoyed his walks by the way he strutted his stuff, gliding along on his toes, his tail held loosely and confidently upright. However, at the sound of Greg's voice, he stopped abruptly and turned in that direction. He was not happy about this intrusion.

So apparently Greg did live next door after all. He repeated this behavior the next day as Faust and I bicycled around the neighborhood. Every morning for four days he appeared in his yard to call a greeting to us as we went by. I no longer felt complimented by his attention. He was surveilling us and I didn't like it.

The beginning of the next week, he once again appeared from behind the house as we were strolling by. But this time Greg came striding across his lawn to greet us up close and personal. Faust, who was sniffing the grass at that moment, growled as he approached. I wrapped the slack in his leash around my right hand, speculating what this growling was about. Faust never growled ... unless you were a big golden brown bear.

Sounding almost contrite, he said, "I suspect I might have seemed overly enthusiastic when we first met, as I tried to learn all about you. I sometimes do that when I meet a very attractive woman I want to get to know." He smiled shyly. I tried not to roll my eyes. "I really would like to get to know you better because I think we have a lot in common. But I've been so busy with my new company it's been hard for me to have any free time."

I started to ask him what he really wanted but

he steamrolled over me, "My start-up, Rowen Marketing Consultants, is here in Sudbury, on Rt. 20, near Raymond Road. I do all kinds of marketing for small businesses and non-profits. Most of my time lately has been spent in getting my newest project—one I'm sure you'll wholeheartedly approve—off the ground. I'd really like us to get together to talk about it and get your sage advice."

All the time he was speaking, Faust's tail was low. It was fiercely scything the grass. His ears lay back flat, his pupils dilated, and his powerful, thick jaw muscles were set. Staring intently, he became more straight-legged. Slowly he arched his back. His fur stood erect. His tail puffed out. A low rumbling, guttural moan rose from his throat. He hissed, spit, and screamed at Greg. Then his body immediately hunkered closer to the ground. He was ready to leap. Any moment he was going to furiously fly at Greg with his claws and teeth exposed. I restrained him tightly.

I had never seen Faust react this way before toward a person. He was a lover not a fighter. But something had piqued his aggression. I wondered if Greg reminded him of some abusive person from his past. This laid-back cat was locked, loaded, and ready to go for Greg's throat in explosive, blood-letting savagery in only a matter of seconds.

"I think it best to get Faust moving along again." We left. Well, *I* left but Faust kept trying to go back, pulling me, all seven pounds and several gallons of adrenaline straining his leash. He clearly had

Signe Dayhoff

unfinished business and had no intention of being prevented from taking care of it ASAP.

The next morning Greg stopped us as we were cycling by to tell me that his new project was marketing for a regional homeless animal non-profit. "I think it's so great you care for homeless animals and have volunteered so selflessly and charitably, given of your time, money, and effort to help them," he rhapsodized. "As I said, I know nothing about animals which is a small problem right now. I was thinking that since you have experience with rescues, perhaps you could give me a clue about what might appeal to animal devotees like yourself, you know, to motivate them to donate and adopt.

"Also," he paused, looking as if he were slightly embarrassed, "I know next to nothing about non-profit shelters themselves, precisely what they do and how they operate. I'll bet you know all about them and that's why you've, no doubt, been effective in helping them. I particularly want to hear about all the things you've done to help them get the funds they need."

Around my shoulders, Faust's body tensed, his pupils contracted. In my peripheral vision I saw him lift one side of his upper lip to scowl at Greg. His claws were puncturing my skin. At this rate, I wasn't going to have any flesh left on my shoulders. I found myself tensing too. Since he obviously knew about my pro bono marketing work with one or two animal shelters in the past, why was he pussy-

209

footing around and still unctuously spreading the butter on with a trowel?

Chagrined, I knew unequivocally he was angling to learn what marketing approaches, strategies, and tactics I had used successfully to help provide a few animal rescue organizations with visibility, funding, and adoptions. But where was he going with this? Did he want to hire me as a consultant? Perhaps, I thought, if I shared some info about shelter needs and issues, I'd get a clue.

I said, "As you may imagine, it's tough to keep up a steady stream of money going to the homeless animal shelters. While they depend primarily on donations from the public, they sometimes can get grants from pet food and other pet supplies manufacturers, foundations, health care, psychological, and civic organizations, pet store franchises, and human-animal bond groups. This means grant writing is an important and useful skill." Faust was stiffening his body in protest.

Greg pursed his lips. "This particular non-profit does a lot of bake sales, garage sales, auctions, pictures with Santa, and contests which, they've indicated, haven't been all that profitable. What else could they do?"

"Everyone does those sorts of things. Unfortunately, they barely make a dent in the financial outlay for housing, feeding, providing medical care for the rescued animals, publicizing, and finding adoptive and foster parents. They need to explore more strategically-planned, viable ways to increase funding."

Faust's body was becoming stiffer as I still straddled the bike at the side of the street. He patted my cheek with his right front paw as if to say, "I want to leave *now*. We're supposed to be riding around the block. Let's get a move on." I petted his head to indicate we'd be leaving shortly.

"I should take Faust on his ride."

"Come on back after you do. I want us to talk some more about this."

As I put my foot on the pedal, Faust licked my right ear for acceding to his wishes. It took several blocks before Faust began to unclench, stretching his legs, and jutting his chin out to feel the wind in his fur. However, as we arrived back home, he appeared to know I was going out again and, this time, without him. He did not like it and showed his annoyance by struggling to stay on my shoulders for as long as possible. He knew I couldn't leave as long as he hung on me like a wet heavy wool sweater, each paw clinging independently.

After carefully, painfully unhooking and re-unhooking every single claw, I placed him on the kitchen floor with his dish bearing kitty treats. He sat staring at me, not touching his dish. So I went into the living room to put some 18th Century classical harp music, performed by Spanish harpist Nicandor Zabaleta, on the stereo. Even though he loved harp music, this time he chose not to follow me. Generally when I put it on, he would sit quietly by the turntable, his tail swaying to the music. In lieu of that he gave me a squinty-eyed, dirty look. I didn't apologize as I slipped back out. His demeanor told me that it didn't matter if it was business or not. Furthermore, when I returned, I'd probably find him sitting on the kitchen counter with upper cabinet doors open, chucking plastic jars of spices onto the floor ... or much worse.

I walked back to Greg's where he invited me to sit in one of the two white wicker chairs he'd brought into his side yard. No sooner had I sat down than he gushed, "You sound as though you know all about helping animal shelters get funding. I really wish I had your knowledge and experience. It would be so helpful to what I'm doing. I really want to help this non-profit help all the animals in need that it can but I feel at such a disadvantage without that knowledge and experience. I'm sure you agree they need *all* the help they can get *however* they can manage to get it."

I frowned at his soft-soaped, not-so-subtle suggestion. I was about to ask Greg what he had done in marketing before coming to Sudbury when he asked, "Since you graciously have done so much, as a volunteer, to help these shelters financially, what specifically have you done to promote them? I mean, have you used articles, brochures, interviews, videos, cable, events, or anything else in particular, in any particular way? You have so much relevant knowledge. I know I can learn so much from you."

Good grief! At this rate this little toady was going

to give himself a hernia pumping me for marketing information. He was no longer bothering to pretend not to know what I had done for these shelters. At least that was an improvement, I guess. Suddenly a flash bulb flashed in my head. Since it was looking less like he was going to ask me to be his consultant, though clearly he desperately needed one on this project, I should propose it. He had the contract but I had the desired know-how. I decided to do my song and dance first to show him how valuable I would be to him, and that he needed me, before I made my proposal.

"Occasionally I have socialized rescued cats to prepare them for adoption to loving homes. Some very good stories have come out of those activities as well as their rescues, some of which have been hair-raising. People love funny, suspenseful, or heartwarming cat stories. I've done interviews for local TV stations with some of the cats and articles for local and regional papers about many of the shelter's interesting activities and unusual situations they'd encountered."

"That's great. Give me some details of exactly what you've done."

"Let me give you a plan I designed for the Delta Society which deals with pet therapy for humans, one that could have been a great national story. One of its members was a pilot who had broken a number of flying records and planned on breaking another one by flying cross-country from the farthest points in the U.S., that is, northeast to southwest and northwest to southeast, with her dog as 'co-pilot.'"

"You've worked nationally too. Even better," he interjected.

"However, the date of the flight was postponed several times for a number of reasons, leaving the event up in the air, so to speak. Consequently, I began by writing several articles about the scheduled trip and its relationship to the human-animal bond for the national and regional press. Of course, this was not the ideal way to start. But given the situation, there was an off-chance it might create some visibility and credibility for pet therapy specifically and interest for when the flight actually would take place. It would also give magazines their needed five-to-six-month lead time."

"So what were you going to do?"

"The plan was to produce articles during and after the flights. These would include lots of photos of her plane and her dog, quotations from people where she landed, other flying celebrities, and celebrities interested in animals. There would be film coverage of her landings. If she won any honors for breaking any records by these flights, there would be press coverage and ceremonial shots. Each article in a series of articles would have been tied into different aspects of the benefits of the human-animal bond, especially pet therapy, like the physical and emotional effects of simply having and caring for a pet. It was designed for the particular ongoing needs of national papers, broadcast news, and magazines."

"Interesting," he smiled. "But I'd really be interested in the ins and outs and the final results you achieved on projects that *did* work out."

I shook my head. I had just provided him a strategy and loads of specific, effective tactics which he could use in any number of ways, with a little ingenuity and creativity, as a basis for numbers of different promotions.

But, as if not having heard a word I said, he merely reiterated, "What worked for you could give me such a big leg up. You know, new business, new project. I can't tell you how great it is that you're an expert and so generous to give me a friendly hand with it. I don't know what I'd do without it ... and you."

He couldn't seem to cease pouring it on thick. I marveled at how he seemed to think he could blithely fawn all over me and manipulate me into sharing all my marketing experience and expertise on the subject, ideas, suggestions, approaches, plans, contacts, strategies, tactics, and feedback ... and all for free.

Greg wanted my professional help. So could I get him to pay for it? Before broaching the subject, I wanted to make clear to him that I, likewise, was a business person who provided marketing consultation ... for a fee. Whatever I had done personally for some non-profit shelters in the past had been as a charitable contribution, as distinct from my regular paid contractual work. I had to be assertively clear that I was not willing to share my marketing methods gratis with him so he could use them for his own for-profit business.

"For many years my business has provided marketing communications consulting to small and large companies nation-wide, like Allergan Pharmaceuticals, for example. For them I created a mailer targeting physicians to promote the use of Allergan's 'Lacrilube' eye ointment for their patients during surgery. I have been *hired* by both for-profit and non-profit organizations."

I let it hang there to see if he would choose to hear and accept that we were professional marketing peers plying our trade for money. But all he said was, "You're amazing. You've done so much. I can't wait to hear more about your successful campaigns."

I exhaled deeply. This would require a different approach, I thought, but not right now. I looked at my watch. "I have a coaching client scheduled in ten minutes. I need to go back home to prepare."

Still unhappy with me when I returned, Faust quietly lay in the center of my desk, spread out on top of the client's file, preventing me from opening it, as I took the call. With prompting he finally moved, albeit reluctantly. At least he hadn't emptied the kitchen cabinet, torn the article I was working on out of my typewriter and rendered it confetti, or flushed his Wiffle Ball down the toilet. As a cat companion, I believe in being thankful for small things.

Later that week Greg saw me with Faust as we walked by. He walked over and gravely began a well-rehearsed, emotional full-court press. "As you know, helping this homeless animal shelter is critically important to me because they do so much for many hundreds of animals which have absolutely no one. These are sad, lonely, frightened, anxious, homeless animals, barely living by their wits on the streets, eating garbage, at risk of being poisoned or attacked by cruel humans or other animals, or struck by cars. They've been abandoned and forgotten. They're wretched refuse. Some have been horribly abused or just plain neglected. Some are sick and hurt. But they're all traumatized. They need our compassion, our caring, our time, and all our supreme effort. They have so much to give yet ask so little. And all they want is to be adopted, cared for, and loved. That's why *you and I* need to help them."

Before I could roll my eyes, a siren whooped side my head. My jaw dropped. I couldn't believe it. He actually had the chutzpah to paraphrase to me a newspaper column I had written over two years ago. Was that supposed to be a compliment or, more likely, was he pretending these were his own thoughts? Tsk, tsk, tsk. It's not nice to fool Mother Nature.

"That's why," he said, "it's so great to talk with someone who as a volunteer knows all about their serious situation and cares *so* deeply about helping them in any way possible to get them a better life. I'd like you to have lunch with me tomorrow so we

217

can discuss it further."

The idea didn't enthrall me. But I still wanted to see if it were worth my while to try to persuade him, despite his obvious resistance, to take me on as a paid consultant. The work for the shelter could be a relatively short job, depending upon what the shelter had contracted for, and IF he had any competence. I was increasingly doubtful about that. Torn, I agreed.

The next day I left Faust home which, again, did not please him. I couldn't wait to see what he would do next to show his annoyance. I met Greg one o'clock in Wayland on Rt. 27 at a small, rustic restaurant which was part of an expansive plant nursery and up-scale farm stand. Strangely, the conversation didn't commence until lunch was being served. When I arrived, Greg was pre-occupied with an eight-and-a-half-by-eleven pad of paper on which he was frantically jotting things. He acknowledged my arrival with a raised pen and nod but continued to write notes and draw figures, only taking a moment out to order, until our meals arrived. I suspected this was to try to impress me somehow. I was not impressed.

He said, "I'm sure you understand that I had to get my ideas down while they were fresh. I was working on a whiz-bang brochure design for the shelter. Tell me about how you've used brochures successfully for achieving what the shelters want."

I sighed and chuckled to myself, drawing some enjoyment from what I was about to say. He wasn't going to like it. "I've found brochures in general to be only one method, among many, in a well-designed, education-based promotional plan, for making an entity's important service, and/or product, known. But for some organizations, like rescue shelters, I've found brochures to be much less important, perhaps even irrelevant and cost-ineffective in general, even for accompanying grant proposals."

"Oh, *really?*" He sounded irritated. "So what else do *you* do besides simply writing articles for your animal non-profits?" He brusquely pushed his pad and pen aside on the table.

It was obvious he had chosen not to take the hint about our both being business people who provide marketing consultation so I'd have to spell out in one-syllable words my position regarding this potential marketing relationship.

"Greg, You have shown considerable interest in what I can provide you marketing-wise in order for you to fulfill your paying contract to help this shelter. As a professional with marketing experience with non-profit animal shelters, I would be happy to help you further but *only* as a paid consultant."

He covered his lower jaw collapse and gaping mouth with, "Well, of course, it would be great if we could work together. I'd really enjoy that." He smiled and reached over to patronizingly pat my hand lying on the table. "But you know," he stated solemnly, nodding, "animal shelters are *not* wealthy."

I had to roll my eyes at his half-witted deflection. The shelter had already paid him and he would pay me for my consultation out of his fee. For my fee I would contribute to his success and he could and would take full credit, something he could then use for gaining other contracts. I moved my hand and asked, "Does that mean you're ready to hire me?"

"You know," he began with his brow furrowed, "I didn't expect ...," he paused. "Actually," he took a deep breath, "I'm really surprised by what you've said." He began taking a different tack. "All this time we've been talking about rescue shelters, and what you did as a volunteer, I thought we were sharing as *friends*. Sharing is what friends do. But what you're suggesting doesn't sound very friendly to me." He shook his head. "However," he pursed his lips, looking serious, "since it apparently is so very important to you to be paid—as distressing as it is to me—I'll do you the favor off giving it some thought."

He took a sip of wine and had a bite of his cheese- and grilled onion-laden steak burger. "In the meantime, while I'm considering your proposal, I need to get a better idea of what you have done successfully. Specifically, what would you say have been your most effective strategies and tactics for getting donations for these shelters?"

Even before I had had a bite of my salmon salad, I signaled the wait staff for a doggie bag for it. Greg stared at me somewhat astonished. I left my half of the bill plus my tip on the table, stood, and before I left, said with a forbearance one would use with an obstreperous young child, "Now, Greg, I've already shared numbers of successes, strategies, and tactics with you. If you want me to continue, you have to pay me for it. It's up to you."

Faust greeted my return with shredded toilet paper adorning his body. "That's not very conservation-minded," I called to him as I carried a broom, dust pan, and garbage bag into the bathroom decorated with white streamers.

A few days later Greg called wanting us to get together for lunch again but made no comment about contracts. I had been more tolerant of his effrontery than he deserved and wasn't willing to play his game any longer. I refused. A few days later he called me again to have us meet over lunch.

"Look, Greg. There's no reason for us to get together unless we're discussing the details of a contract. If you don't want to hire me, just come out and say so."

"I'm honestly surprised at you," he replied. "As a friend, I don't think what you're *demanding* is very friendly."

"If we're being honest and telling it as it is, Greg, we're not friends. We're acquaintances, and barely that."

It had become all too evident that I was masochistically butting my head against a brick wall. I needed to step back to ask myself if I really wanted to work with him. He didn't seem professional, experienced, or particularly knowledgeable. Furthermore, he'd shown me no evidence he was ethical or trustworthy.

"Why do women have to be so emotional?" He hung up. Being more mature, I stuck out my tongue at the phone.

The next day as I was jogging by Greg's, he ran out to me. He had a pen and a pad of paper in hand and acted as if we had never had our last conversation. "I was thinking about what you said about brochures and I think you're wrong about not using them for rescue shelters. I have a couple of questions about them."

If I had thought he might have finally recognized that all his clever maneuvering wasn't going to work, I was quickly disabused of that notion. I shook my head, incredulous. There was no way I was ever going to bet on him. He was a bad pony.

"Greg, look at it this way. It's the top of the ninth, the bases are loaded. You've had a chance to hit one out of the park to win the game but you've chosen to strike out."

For a moment he seemed nonplussed, then angry. Regrouping, as I started to jog off, he replayed his broken record. I stopped for the last time.

"You know," he whined, "I was honestly under the impression that your interest was, as it has been before, in *voluntarily* helping these non-profit animal shelters because you know the great importance of the work they do. But, apparently, I was mistaken about your commitment to them.

"As for me paying you? Why should I? You have helped them before for no pay. It seems to me this would simply be a continuation of what you have done for them in the past. I can't tell you how disappointing, disheartening, and distasteful it is to hear from someone as allegedly caring as you that it's no longer about doing the right, compassionate thing. No, you've evidently become hardened and greedy. Now it's only about the money."

I smiled, looked him in the eye, and shrugged my shoulders. His handsome face took on an expression of disbelief as if I had suggested roasting babies with potatoes, carrots, and onions.

Seemingly unable to quit, he tried it again, upping his game. "That's so mercenary, so selfish. Haven't you even a hint of compassion for all these poor, desperate animals which will die without the shelter's help? No, you can only think about yourself ... and *money*, instead of helping me make their lives better. That's disgusting and just plain pathetic. You should be ashamed of yourself!"

I couldn't help grinning, which probably wasn't the best thing to do in that circumstance. What I really wanted to do was laugh out loud. What *was* truly pathetic were his attempts to make me feel guilty. It's a psychological truism that when nothing else works, people out to take advantage of you unfailingly whip out the guilt trip. They blame, belittle, and shame you, hoping this denigrating trio will force you to feel remorse, and give in, for having had the unmitigated gall to ask for what you legitimately wanted. I regarded his face this last time as I began to leave.

"I truly wish that animal shelter much success," I said. "But sadly, I suspect, what they're going to need is a *lot* of luck." I jogged away. All his first-encounter superficial charm had trickled away, leaving a good-looking but hollow, rapidly-decaying shell.

From that day forward Greg didn't appear in his yard when Faust and I went by. Faust seemed particularly pleased about that, likely thinking his behavior was what had precipitated this hoped for change. I suspected Faust had immediately sensed something about Greg that I was much slower to discover.

It was only now that I admitted to myself that when he first appeared on my door step, my juices began flowing. In those first-glance seconds my estrogen and progesterone had spiked to conjure up what it would have been like if we had been the major characters in a hot romantic movie. Meeting by chance, this Robert Redford-clone and I would have been drawn to each other as destiny-intended soul mates. And before long, Panther Boy and I would have been locked in a sweaty, heaving, surging, pulsating, inwardly-downwardly full nelson on the Oriental. Ah, the joys of a hormone-inspired imagination.

18

STRIPPER'S REMORSE

Claudia Smissman called a week later to say she had found another small house, about 1,125 sq. ft. to rent and asked if I'd like to see it. It was in west Framingham in a 1960s "Rambling Ranch" development off Oak Hill Road, below the Massachusetts Turnpike and Route 9. It was farther out than I wanted but time was slipping away and I needed to explore all reasonable avenues. Faust and I in the interim had gone to more unsuccessful Open Houses than I wanted to think about. I really didn't want to rent an apartment. Today Faust and I met Claudia at her office at 10 a.m. and we followed her to the property.

It was a disappointing one-story with a low-pitched gray roof, vertical siding painted barn red, two large horizontal windows trimmed in white that faced the street, with an attached white garage sporting small windows across the top of the door for decoration. The front yard was postage stamp with only a passing recollection of grass. It didn't even rise to the level of "shabby chic." As I soon found upon inspection, the interior of the house wasn't much better than the outside. While not in disrepair, it simply looked past its prime and no longer loved. It required more TLC, time, and effort than I was willing to devote to revitalizing a rental.

Claudia said, "I know it isn't sharp but minimally you could have the landlord paint the interior. Maybe she would even agree to seeding the front lawn. However, I doubt she'd go to the expense of having sod put in."

Sod? I repeated to myself. Give me a break. This whole property—house and yard—needed a total cosmetic makeover involving serious face-lift surgery and liposuction. Sod alone wasn't going to turn this distressed, and distressing, property into anything remotely attractive and inviting.

"You could brighten it up with art, areas rugs, and colorful curtains," Claudia added. I stifled a sigh and nodded my half-hearted agreement.

As we finished the tour, which included worn, traffic-patterned dark blue shag carpet throughout, we stood in the cookie-cutter kitchen. Faust sat on the worn red Formica counter near the sink. He was gazing out the window onto the fenced, treeless, dirt-patched backyard which still boasted a ramshackle dog house and piles of petrified dog feces. This was a dispiriting come down from what Faust's current yard offered.

We'd said all we had to say about the property when Claudia asked confidentially, "Can I share something with you? I mean, it has nothing to do with this house or real estate. But it's bothering me and I need some professional feedback."

Uh-oh, I thought, the old "professional feedback" gambit. That was code for asking for help resolving a problem but not wanting to hire me to do it. Because I was a psychologist, consultant, and coach, I was constantly being asked to solve peoples' problems ... to instantly, magically pull the right answer out of the air to save them ... and, of course, do it for free. After all, having therapy, psychological consulting, or coaching required time, money, motivation, and, most of all, lots of personal effort. Better to go the fast-food route by asking a casual question in a social setting. Cocktail parties, which were well-lubricated with alcohol, were best for approaching the question, but nearly any occasion would do if you knew how to catch the professional off-guard.

Usually when put in this situation, I explained that to explore and discover their *true* underlying problem—not just their symptoms, what the problem "appeared" to be, to see it clearly from every angle, and to help them find the most effective way to address it—I'd need their involvement over an extended period of time. However, in this particular situation, given Claudia's unusual experience with the dancing "Mr. Smiley," I thought this question might be equally unusual. I decided to give her fifteen minutes. Maybe a few well-placed questions from me might help get her looking more objectively at whatever this "problem" was. I said, "So tell me what's bothering you."

Her whole body changed. Suddenly her shoulders-back-look of confidence was gone. She seemed to sag onto herself. In place of this usually assertive, all-business woman was a troubled, seemingly insecure, awkward teenager. Claudia had difficulty finding a place to start.

"I had gone to an exotic dance club in Boston, one of the less seedy ones, I think, with several woman friends. I mean, I'd never been to one before. You know, we did it as a lark. We were sitting at a table, drinking ... well, I had a Coke ... watching how the men behaved as well as what the dancers did. I mean, you could do a whole sociologic study on men's behavior in such places ... you know, what dances worked and what didn't." She paused. She was taking her time setting the stage.

"As I understand it, you know, in some clubs the dancers totally strip. In some they're topless but wear a G-string. In the club we visited, all the girls finished with G-strings and pasties or scanty bikini-type outfits." Claudia giggled uncomfortably.

She continued, "I was surprised how important the shoes and clothing were. I mean, there were definite styles. One dancer looked like a little girl. You know, wearing a short pink dress with bows and barrettes, ankle socks, Mary Jane shoes, and her hair in braids. That was a little weird. It made me think of pedophiles in the audience. Then there was an edgier look. You know, tight leather, some chains, lots of hair and harsh makeup, trying to look like a female in a Hell's Angels motorcycle gang. I mean, it was sort of an in-your-face rough-sex feel. What I liked best were the dancers with the more sensual, long-flowing, satin or silk gown look. I mean, everything about them looked sexy but classy."

I nodded and said, "Uh huh," to acknowledge I had heard her. Faust was stretching, getting restless. He looked at the sink faucet as if to ask for a drink. I turned on a thin stream of water which he dreamily began to slurp, managing to get his face wet, whiskers dripping, in the process.

"Anyway," Claudia said, "I was always trying to find ways to please Arthur. You know, he's my boyfriend and I'm crazy about him. You know, he's a prominent anesthesiologist at Brigham and Women's Hospital. We've been together for six months now. As I watched the dancers, I thought maybe I could create, you know, a sexy dance for him. But I realized that would actually be very tough for me because I grew up in a household where exotic dancers were, you know, thought of as sluts and 'nice girls' didn't even pretend to be strippers. But I knew Arthur had gone to strip clubs with his doctor friends. I thought, you know, he would get a kick out of my 'dancing sexy' for him."

At this point Faust jumped down from the counter and began checking out the living room on his own. After I turned off the tap, Claudia and I followed his lead as she went on with her story. "It took me weeks to get the swaying and gliding moves right, I mean, no bumps and grinds. And then, you know, I had to find a floor-length nightgown and robe of the same flowing, delicate material. I settled

on a black silk, low-cut gown with a slit up to here."
She pointed to her hip. "I mean, it was hard to find.
I also got a black silk robe with lace at the top.
Under the gown I had on, you know, a tiny lacy
black strapless bra and G-string." Looking off into
space, Claudia appeared to be reliving her
preparations.

"The night of my exotic dance performance
Arthur came over for dinner, as he usually did.
After we finished our wine sitting on the sofa, I
excused myself, you know, for a moment, so I could
dress in my costume. I put Ravel's *Bolero* on the
stereo. Anxiously I stepped out from the bedroom
holding one side of the robe and swept by him. You
know, it was something like what Lili St. Cyr did
seductively in burlesque. I'd seen her do an erotic
routine at a production of "That Was Burlesque"
that came to Framingham's old Carousel Theater
years ago.

"As I danced around the room in time to the
music, you know, as gracefully as I could, I used
the fabric of the gown to accentuate my body. I
slowly inched out of my robe letting it fall to the
carpet. Then casually dropping one shoulder than
the other of the gown, I danced until I was wearing
next to nothing. You know, I was so proud of myself
for having thought of it for him and having had the
guts to execute it as flawlessly as I could manage. I
mean, I had rehearsed and rehearsed."

Faust had crawled up onto the living room sofa,
the only piece of furniture in the room, and

kneaded the floral cream-and-tan, heavy cotton fabric seat cushion as if waiting for me to sit down with him. When I didn't immediately respond, he looked up at me, waved his right paw in the air, and looked down at the cushion again. Claudia and I sat on the sofa and he crawled onto my lap, curling up. "Go on," I prompted her.

"When I finished, I was smiling, feeling great, even sexy, you know. But he looked at me as if I were like something from a 1950s horror film. My heart squeezed tight. I mean, I didn't understand. Suddenly I felt queasy. I turned off the stereo. He stated that he was 'shocked' by my performance. He said I ought to be 'ashamed' of myself. You know, I felt like a bad little girl who had done something so awful, I mean, that even punishment wasn't enough. He said what I'd done looked just plain 'stupid.' You know, I wanted to die as I stood there in front of him, nearly nude." Claudia looked as if she were about to cry. I put my hand on hers and waited. Faust moved onto her lap and kneaded her thighs, purring.

"I was humiliated beyond words. You know, I'd struggled to do something I would never ordinarily have done, thinking it would please him. But somehow I'd gotten the wrong message. I mean, I guess he liked exotic dancers but not me doing an exotic dance. You know, I just didn't get it. But I knew never to do anything like it ever again.

"After a while, he stopped looking at me as if I were the *Creature from the Black Lagoon* or the village idiot. Over time I think he forgave me or, you know, he seemed to have decided that I was someone he could associate with without embarrassment. So a couple of weeks later we took a weekend vacation in Las Vegas. He had some kind of medical conference he was attending and said he wanted company. You know, I was so psyched. I'd have a lot of time to myself while he was in seminars and I couldn't wait to do everything that Vegas is so famous for. I mean, I was making all kinds of fun plans.

"However, as soon as we arrived, he stated that drinking and gambling were 'out.' 'Out?' I mean, I don't know what he expected I'd do. Get roaring drunk and sell myself body and soul at the craps table? You know, I've never drunk more than one glass of wine, and that's only with dinner, and have never gambled. That was, you know, shocking but even more disappointing because that's part of Vegas night life. You know, stay up late and check everything out. You know," she laughed, "they say, 'What happens in Vegas stays in Vegas.' I mean, I'm in my late thirties and live a somewhat staid life. This was going to be exciting and glamorous. I mean, I was *really* looking forward to it. Then he said that the only activities that were 'in' were shows and dinner. Crummy shows and dinner? Big whoop-dee-do!" Claudia circled her index finger in the air and exhaled deeply as if fighting back tears. Faust snuggled closer to her.

"Making matters worse," she said, "he wouldn't let me touch him, sexually or otherwise, *after* 10:30

p.m. I mean, what was that about? He stated he 'should' be sleeping at that hour. But even in Las Vegas? So why had he bothered to take me there with him? I mean, I could just as easily have stayed home and, you know, had as much 'fun' playing with my bulldog, Winston, going to movies, or having pizza with the girls." She looked more confused and peeved than sad.

When Claudia finished, Faust bunted her chest and licked her arm as if to comfort her in her disconsolation. Unfortunately I'd seen Arthur's type of behavior before. I'd also experienced it first-hand. To fulfill my end of our agreement I started asking Claudia a few neutral questions I wanted her to ponder to hopefully open up some paths for her reflection.

"What was there about Arthur that initially attracted you?"

She smiled and said, "He was good looking, had a good job, and seemed interested in me."

"How did he show his interest?"

"He talked about how attractive I was and how he liked my body. We clicked. I mean, we had sex on the first date. It was good and, you know, we do it nearly every time he comes by to see me."

"Tell me about yourself. Specifically, what are your strengths, interests, values? What makes you feel good?"

Claudia thought a minute, "Well," she said, "you know, I'm a good realtor. I mean, I can generally read clients and what they really want and successfully match properties to them. As a result, I make a decent living. I have, you know, lots of friends, not just realtors, and I enjoy doing things with them—I mean, all kinds of activities, from a cup of coffee together to working for some charity or cause. I like movies, comedies and some dramas. You know, like *Back to the Future, Prizzi's Honor*, and *Silkwood*. I read thrillers most often. I used to collect and read Robin Cook's novels but, you know, Arthur says his books are medical 'trash.' I like picnics and going to the beach and love dancing. You know, I love my dog. Oh, and I run. Those are the things that make me feel good."

"What does Arthur like to do?"

"Well, he's very busy so when he comes over in the evening, you know, he's often too tired to do much. We have dinner—generally he provides me with the recipes he likes which I have to follow closely—and then, you know, a quick roll in the hay. You know, he has never stayed over at my place and usually leaves early. We don't go to movies very often because, you know, he says he finds American movies to be too childish or lacking in substance. I mean, he prefers foreign-language films at the Orson Welles Cinema in Cambridge because of their 'artistry.' But, you know, they often leave me cold. I mean too much 'artistry' and too little story and action.

"He likes to read. Of course, he's always reading medical journals. He says that when he reads fiction, which he stresses isn't often, you know, he reads only 'intellectually stimulating' fiction. One book he really likes is Umberto Eco's *The Name of the Rose*. He says it's because the book combines 'semiotics,' whatever that is, and all kinds of 'historical, biblical, philosophical, and literary references.' I tried reading it but it didn't hold my interest. It seemed to me as if it were trying too hard to be clever. But I'm no literary expert.

"He's not a beach or picnic person. He doesn't dance, or, at least, he's never taken me dancing when I've asked him to. He goes to his gym and plays handball. He doesn't run and says, you know, he doesn't understand my preoccupation with it.

"Winston drives him crazy. You know, he thinks my dog snuffles, licks himself all the time, and smells. He says he finds him 'revolting.' You know, he suggested once that I get rid of Winston because he doesn't like having him around. Of course, I never would. I mean, I've had Winston since he was a puppy and I love him dearly. He's family. I once suggested that since he didn't want to be around Winston, you know, we could go to his home instead—we never had. But he has said no." Faust rubbed his face in her lap and continued to purr.

"Tell me, how would your ideal mate behave toward you? That is, how would he treat you?"

"Ideal? Ha! You mean if there were such a thing? Well, theoretically, he'd be interested in what I'm interested in, you know, big things and little things. I don't mean he'd be *just* like me. No, I mean, we'd talk and share thoughts. You know, each of us would accept what the other says without judgment. He'd be smart, funny, and compassionate, you know, really caring about people and their feelings. Of course, he'd respect me and my decisions and, you know, appreciate all I do, especially whatever I do for him. And, I guess, he'd be proud of me too. But nobody can or does find that. Nobody. So why bother even thinking about it."

"Claudia, You've described a situation that bothers you. So what do you see *the* problem is that you want to solve?"

She paused, raising her eyebrows then frowning. A minute passed. "I'm not sure, I guess," she paused again looking uncomfortable. "Well, maybe I just wanted to, you know, complain to someone. I mean, I haven't shared this with my girlfriends. They wouldn't understand." I was sure she was right about that and that they'd probably give her an earful she wouldn't want to hear.

"Tell me if this sounds about right to you. From what you've said it sounds to me as if you have some questions about your relationship with Arthur, perhaps if it's making you feel the way you want. What do you think?" Claudia frowned again but said nothing.

"On the chance you might wish to explore this possibility, given what you value in yourself and in an ideal mate, you might find it useful to think about how Arthur compares with your ideal mate on a scale of 1 to 10, with one being *not at all* and ten being *totally*." Claudia narrowed her eyes and her lips tightened. She didn't respond at first. Minutes passed.

"You mean," Claudia finally asked, "that *aside* from his being smart, with a high-status job and good pay, and being good in bed?"

"Yes. It might be useful to see how you feel he matches with those other things you've stated you personally value, like, and want."

Claudia looked aghast for an instant at what she probably perceived as a challenge she didn't like. It was palpable she was asking herself, "What is she implying? Is she saying there is something wrong with Arthur? Is she saying I shouldn't be with him? Is she suggesting I've made a bad choice in staying with him?"

Scowling, she looked as if she sorely wished she hadn't asked me for help. And what, she was likely wondering, had possessed her to share such intimate details of her life with me, a potential client? I could see her emotionally hitting her forehead. Furthermore, now she was being asked to inspect what she did not want to explore, seriously or otherwise. The risk was too great. I could see her body tension now revealing feelings of conflict, anger, and fear.

She chose to say nothing—not about my taking my time to listen to her, not about my providing feedback to her, and not about her intentions to even consider thinking about any of it. I guessed that unless something earthshaking happened to change her mind to the contrary, she'd probably continue with the status quo, irrespective of how she felt in her current relationship and what she wished for instead.

I mentally shrugged. She'd had her fifteen minutes of "therapeutic fame." It was time to disengage. Faust crawled up her front, rubbed his cheek against her chest, and licked her neck. With a muted smile I said, "Thanks for the preview but I think this house needs a bit more work than I want to put in on a rental." As I arose from the sofa, Faust jumped down and sidled up next to me. I gently lifted him and wrapped him around my neck.

After a moment, Claudia rose as well. Slowly she seemed to regain her business stature and walked toward the front door with me behind her. Once outside, I waited as she closed and locked the door and returned the key to the lock box. Then she turned in my general direction and said, jaw clenched, "I'm not sure we have anything a little newer, smaller, or requiring less work for you." She didn't make eye contact.

"I appreciate the time and effort you've spent with me," I offered to which she merely nodded.

We left in our respective cars, she toward her office and Faust and I toward home. I strongly suspected I wouldn't hear from her about real estate after this interaction. I likewise assumed she wouldn't contact me about her "problem." I exhaled deeply and lamented that Faust and I had to keep house hunting.

Knowing better, I also wished people would stop asking me for what they didn't want to think about, much less do anything about. Change was a threatening unknown, a tough and frightening exploratory process, often not one for the unsure or fainthearted.

19

CALIFORNIA YEARNING

At least it had been a clear, sunny day with only a few thin clouds skipping across the baby-blue sky. After Claudia's rental preview, it was late afternoon and the traffic was increasing on Route 9 as we approached Framingham Center. With Faust settled around my neck, we were taking our time heading back to Sudbury, to pick up Edgell Road across from Framingham State College (now Framingham State University). I had fond memories about what the college had done for me when I returned from Baylor University, no longer able to financially continue with my pre-med studies.

I was in the left lane doing 45 mph, keeping pace with a furniture truck that was just ahead on my right fender. I was planning to stop at the pharmacy at Temple Street intersection, three quarters of a mile ahead on the right. Consequently, when traffic allowed, I slowed and pulled in behind the truck to prepare to exit.

Simultaneously, a red Chevy Malibu charged out of the Friendly's Ice Cream shop parking lot on the right. It barreled into the traffic, aimed at a slot behind the truck ... which I had just occupied.

Unless he acted immediately, the driver would accordianize his car ... and render himself roadkill. Faust and I would be collateral damage as the Rabbit caromed off other cars like the cue ball in game of billiards.

He slammed on the brakes. The car stopped. But the front of his sporty car was already half-way into my lane. With no time to check I swerved sharply to the left. Faust was thrown against the closed driver's side window. He hit with a splat. Butt first. Then his head connected with the glass. Only seconds previously a green Ford sedan had vacated the left lane. I had lucked out. But a pick-up truck was rapidly approaching. I sharply swerved to the right. I slid by the Malibu within five inches of his headlights.

Everything was happening in slow-motion. Faust glided through the air, thrown to the floor of the passenger side. I heard him grunt. A moment later, my right directional signal clicked on. The Rabbit glided into the pharmacy's parking lot.

Undoubtedly bruised, Faust appeared only a little worse for wear. Incredibly he was still conscious but groggy. He shook his head. Unfastening my seat belt, I reached over and pulled up the passenger door latch button. I opened my door and dashed around to the passenger's side. I leaned in, gently picked him up, and placed him on the seat. Talking to him, I carefully examined his body. He continued to shake his head.

After a few minutes, I put him on the ground to

see if he could stand and walk without difficulty. He listed a little to the left. Then to my great relief he did manage to put one paw in front of the other and keep his balance. Carefully I wrapped him around my neck—I didn't want to leave him in the car, just in case he'd lose consciousness without me there— and walked quickly into the pharmacy. As soon as we arrived home, I called Dr. Bridges for an appointment, to do x-rays, if necessary. After that concussive blow to his head, I'd have to closely observe him for the next several days, irrespective of whatever the films showed.

Despite my compulsion to do so, I didn't want to replay in my mind how close we had come. That it had been only a matter of seconds—a simple toss of the dice. This time I'd thrown a seven. Luck had been with me. I was so thankful Faust wasn't seriously hurt. But, I considered, if he hadn't been around my neck, perhaps he might not have been hurt at all.

Time passed quickly as I finished with several coaching clients, another article for *Boston Business Journal*—"Working to Stay on the Cutting Edge," and continued to check out house rentals, as we edged ever closer to Tom and Molly's return. Faust's x-rays had been negative. He was acting normally, ready to play Wiffle Ball or dazzle me with a new "trick."

In fact, he seemed to be increasingly interested in mimicking actions he saw on television. When he saw a Chinese acrobat lie on his back and balance and roll a large ball on his feet, Faust appeared to try to do it. The problem was that the Wiffle Ball wouldn't co-operate with Faust. Lying on his back, when he grabbed it with his front paws, he couldn't transfer it to his back paws. When he could somehow manage to move it toward the rear end of his body, his back paws couldn't seize it. His back legs were either too elevated or improperly angled to provide a level platform. Or his legs were too folded against his abdomen to raise them and move the ball. After a while, he ceased trying, contemptuously pushing the Wiffle Ball aside. Under my watchful eye he pretended to be blasé about it. However, his drooping head and tail suggested he felt disappointed and discouraged.

That mood of exasperation wouldn't, and never did, last long. Faust was always seeking and spotting something new to try. It was like when I was seated on the sofa that he'd lie on his back on my thighs, his body fully stretched out, his head dipping back over my knees, and front legs raised above his head, suspended in space, as I rubbed his tummy. Occasionally, he'd finish the session by sliding smoothly backwards off my knees as if to do a handstand.

At other times he'd climb the wall backwards. With his front legs nearly in a handstand his back legs crawled up the wall on his stomach. I wondered if this was preparation for what he tried next. Away from the wall, he seemed to be attempting to balance on his front legs with his bottom in the air. I recalled our having watched a Cairn terrier achieve this handstand on television.

No question, if I hadn't observed this myself, I would simply not have believed a cat would try to do this. I mean, as far as my skeptical human brain was concerned, cats just didn't do that sort of thing. But, then again, Faust was "smarter than the average bear"—er, "cat"—and always pushing the envelope.

His trying to accomplish the same maneuver from a standing start was a frustrating no-go. His body automatically dropped back to his previous position. And the one time he pushed harder with his rear legs to achieve vertical, it pushed him over. Eyes wide, looking startled, he scrambled to get his head out of the way. With no time to twist his falling body, he tried to tuck himself to soften the blow. But he rolled hard onto his shoulders and back. After the resulting, frightening spinal crunch, he abandoned this folly. I suspect he concluded that it was a dog's inferior anatomy that allowed such a useless exercise. Instead, he returned to trying variations of his backward slide from my knees to the floor.

I contemplated what Faust would do if he ever encountered a skateboard. Ride it, and successfully, of course. In my fantasy I could picture him with his driving gloved front paws poised to make him more aerodynamic, long white silk scarf around his neck, trailing behind him in the breeze, his black leather aviator's open-cockpit helmet buckled under his chin, and his rubber goggles strapped in place, looking something like Snoopy as a World War One flying ace. Considering how difficult it had been to keep Faust in his Dracula costume for Hallowe'en, maybe he would do better skateboarding while kitty-nude. If he were lucky, one of the children on Willow Road would roll by on urethane wheels and provide him with the opportunity to try. However, I had never seen one so that was still possible for the future, before we moved.

The shadow of moving which hung heavily over me reminded me, wistfully, that long before Faust entered my life, my mother and I had made a move from Massachusetts to San Diego. Moving was an adventure in itself. It consisted of pulling a five-by-ten,1,250-pound, U-Haul cargo trailer 3,044 miles, driving over ten hours a day for five days. Taking the wrong entrance back onto the highway after getting gas, we ended up stuck on a dead-end dirt road with ditches on both sides in an isolated area of northern Texas. Extricating ourselves was filled with adrenaline-coated, sweat-infused "excitement."

And to make it all perfect, when we arrived in San Diego, the first apartment that we looked at wouldn't rent to us. The woman manager said, "I don't believe you are mother and daughter. I will not rent to two women who will up to no good. I won't have *your kind* in my apartments." Despite this action being housing discrimination, pure and simple, after so many exhausting days of hard driving, we weren't up to dragging a trailer around the unknown city to find government offices in which to make a complaint. Besides, the very next apartment we saw accepted us in a snap. Fortunately not everyone saw two conservatively-dressed women alone as potential hookers or lesbians. Sadly, we lived there for only one year before returning to Massachusetts.

We were quickly employed but spent many of our off-hours in Balboa Park. The San Diego Zoo was our favorite. It was a pioneer in the concept of open-air and cage-less habitats, with each habitat particularly suited to its inhabitant. While I loved seeing these animals, I hated seeing them captive. But I was glad they had been rescued and might help people appreciate why wild animals needed to be protected and preserved in the wild. Maybe conscientious, technologically-advanced zoos, like San Diego, could also help keep endangered species going.

We were also regular visitors to the San Diego Museum of Art, the Natural History Museum, the many park gardens, and the Old Globe Theater. This wooden replica of the 600-seat Old Globe in London produced modern plays, musicals, Shakespearean plays, and other classics. It was where we saw twenty-six-year-old actor Christopher Walken. Walken had already made a name for himself by being on the daytime drama *Guiding Light*, the cop series *Naked City*, on Broadway in *Lion in Winter*, *Hawaii Five-O*, and in the film, *Me and My Brother*, with Sean Connery. But in 1969 he was playing Marc Antony in *Julius Caesar* for the 20th San Diego National Shakespeare Festival. It was an impressive, enjoyable production.

Both of us commuted to work in beautiful downtown La Jolla. A seven-mile-long hilly, coastal, elite community, it was about fourteen miles north, via Interstate 5, of our apartment on Arizona Street. Mother was employed in the office of an electronics firm on Prospect Street. I worked at what was then called Scripps Clinic and Research Foundation, formerly the Scripps Metabolic Clinic, just a block away from Mother, also on Prospect. In the clinic's endocrinology office, under the supervision of Dr. Thomas H. Lambert, M.D., their diabetes specialist, I handled paperwork for a double-blind clinical research study of an Upjohn oral substitute for insulin treatment.

Besides his research and diabetes work, Dr. Lambert also saw many of the movie industry stars because of Scripps' health care contract for insurance physicals with the studios. I suspect the one movie person I remember most vividly was John Wayne. I saw him, heavy-set and over six-feet tall, walking down the private hallway to Dr. Lambert's office. He was tugging on his too-short hospital gown, attempting unsuccessfully to cover his private parts, muttering, "Oh, shit!"

Perched on a cliff overlooking the ever-changing, sapphire blue Pacific, my office allowed me to watch the waves roar in. They lashed the cliff face, swirled, and exploded in a spectral spray as a result of its many sea-level caves in the north-facing bluffs. I wondered about the origin of the town's name.

According to town lore, it was historically uncertain whether "la jolla" was derived from "la joya" meaning "the jewel," which the area certainly was, or what the local Native Americans, Kumeyaay, referred to as "land of holes."

Even though San Diego was on the coastline, I never thought about the possibility of experiencing anything worse than Massachusetts inland fog. However, highway travel in Southern California was occasionally significantly impacted by shallow, dense marine layer fog along the coastline with visibility down to less than a quarter of a mile. When it moved in, it was always hazardous along the Pacific Coast Highway as well as Interstates 5, 10, 105, 110, 405, and 710. Frighteningly, Mother and I found that out firsthand.

We were returning from Los Angeles on I-5 after a full day of sightseeing, including the beautifully tranquil Japanese Garden in Van Nuys, a disappointing Universal Studios Tour where nothing happened but a cowboy shootout, and intriguing constellation-viewing at the Griffith Observatory's planetarium. Just north of Oceanside, a wall of white waited in ambush to totally engulf us. Blinded, I couldn't see the taillights of the car in front of us until I was nearly on top of its bumper. In spite of this, vehicles were passing us doing fifty and above. I was confounded. I couldn't believe they could see what we couldn't.

As much as we wanted to pull over to the side of the highway to wait out the fog bank, we didn't dare. Being struck from behind and killed as we sat there invisible was practically guaranteed. There was only one thing to do. So when a large, dilapidated, wood-slatted vegetable truck cut in front of us, I gripped the steering wheel, riveted my right foot to the accelerator, threw the transmission into high gear, and zoomed ahead into the nothingness. I told my mother to brace herself as I glued our 1959 two-toned green Ford's headlights to the truck's back lights. We knew we were more than likely going to die horribly ... squished from the rear or kissing the farm truck's engine if it stopped short. Either way it would likely be in a spectacular, fog-dissipating conflagration.

But forty-five minutes later, miraculously, we reached University Avenue in San Diego. Since it had just begun to clear, we were able to catch the lighted large green overhead exit sign in time to make the fast right-hand turn. The truck continued south. Every muscle from my scalp all the way to the toes on my right foot was locked tight, screaming in spasm. Even if I hadn't had the *Guinness Book of World Records*' migraine as a result, I vowed *never again*. No one could pay me enough to re-experience that overwhelming impotence and fear. Flagrantly jeopardizing my own, and my mother's, mortality was not my idea of smart.

Everyone has heard about California earthquakes. Of course, so had we before we moved to San Diego. There were four faults in Southern California alone: San Andreas, San Jacinto,

Elsinore, and Imperial. However, "earthquakes" had been merely an abstraction, hardly worthy of consideration in my thinking as we enjoyed the area. San Diego, after all, wasn't San Francisco or Los Angeles. That is, until the afternoon of September 12, 1970, when an earthquake shook La Jolla. It may have been the consequence of the magnitude 4.0 originating in Lytle Creek, in the San Gabriel Mountains. I never found out for sure.

My mother had just left work to go out to lunch, something she rarely did, mostly brown-bagging it and eating at her desk to save money. I was to join her as soon as I could get away. She was heading down two blocks to the Rathskeller restaurant to check out its German food. This was despite her having been born in Norway and preferring more fishy-fare. Abruptly she was nearly sent sprawling as the sidewalk rolled in waves beneath her feet. She was saved only by a postal box which happened to be nearby. She grabbed on to it and clung helplessly until the undulations subsided.

While she was experiencing the "possible end of the world," I hadn't felt even a hint of the quake. Having been in an elevator going down one level to the Scripps research building, I was totally oblivious to what was happening. As the building swayed, the elevator had damped the shock wave. But when the elevator doors opened, I saw that everyone else on that level was hanging on to the rail along the windowed lower hallway wall. They were shaken up, speculating on the quake's magnitude, if there'd likely be an aftershock, and what that would mean for the evening's commute.

My mother, who had since abandoned her plans for trying Sauerbraten and Black Forest cake, called me as soon as she returned to her office. She detailed her life-reviewing event with alarm. The seismic message had been loud and clear. Earthquakes were no longer an abstraction. They were something we were now forced to keep in mind.

However, it wasn't until September 26, fourteen days later, when a raging wildfire to the east, in the Laguna Mountains area of San Diego Country, radically and ultimately changed our living plans. Up to that moment we had been rationalizing and excusing the previous natural occurrences. But this was a wildfire ... and it wasn't hundreds of miles away. Furthermore, it was racing hell-bent toward us!

Caused by downed power lines and Santa Ana winds—strong, extremely dry, down-sloped inland winds—it blazed westward thirty miles in twenty-four hours. It incinerated everything in its path. Suddenly it had made it all the way to the outskirts of El Cajon, sixteen miles northeast of San Diego. At that time it was the third largest wildfire in California history.

Reddening the skies, the fire covered San Diego with ash rainfall which smothered plants and burned holes in our car's paint job. Its blast-furnace heat made breathing difficult. Restricted to the city, we had to stay indoors and keep our movements to a minimum. In order to sleep, it was necessary to lie on the cooler linoleum kitchen floor, covered with wet dish towels. At that time the apartment complex offered no air-conditioning. Cross ventilation from window placement generally achieved a comfortable temperature, but not now.

This all-encompassing human-, house-, animal-, and plant bonfire gave us a lot of time to think ... and recall the happenings of our past year. This was the third too-close-for-comfort, potential disaster we'd experienced here. We'd left Massachusetts in hopes of starting fresh. We had been in dead-end jobs, barely getting by. My parents had divorced and my father was still struggling with employment and health issues but now living in Florida. My brother, just out of the Navy, had followed him and was working on a fishing boat in the Gulf of Mexico. We wanted—needed—a change of scene. And we'd found it—and loved it—but Nature seemed to be challenging our willingness to face its recurring, dangerous antics. After the impenetrable fog bank and earthquake, the wildfire on steroids was merely the pièce de résistance.

After a week of fiery heat and fear, with firefighting and emergency vehicles having clogged the highways, preventing our egress, the police finally allowed traffic out of the city. Upon serious reconsideration, we sorrowfully decided to head back to Massachusetts. We notified our employers and secured another five-by-ten U-Haul trailer, packed up the few pieces of furniture we had since acquired and our personal belongings, and left heading east.

To our consternation and amazement we discovered the interstate's asphalt was still warm and soft. We had to navigate the roads carefully so as not to get too close to the shoulders for fear of becoming stuck. The sharp fumes of the heated petroleum-based road surface produced headaches, eye irritation, and coughs. On top of that was the revolting sulfurous smell of burned animal hair, as well as that of charred animal flesh and plant life. It all made having the windows open even a crack in the intense heat nauseating.

A decade had softened my disturbing recollection of those natural disasters. I still thought from time to time about Southern California, that maybe I'd like to try living in the Golden State again. Perhaps if those phenomena hadn't occurred so closely together ... Perhaps if each and all of them combined hadn't been life-threatening. Perhaps if we hadn't so recently left such an emotionally stressful situation in Massachusetts ... Perhaps we would have stayed there permanently as we had planned. We had been delighted to have experienced so much natural beauty: from the ocean to the mountains to the desert. No snow or icy windshields. All that glorious sunshine. What more could one ask?

We had loved exploring the Anza-Borrego Desert especially in spring when its cactus-floral display revealed its consummate glory. There were so many varieties of cactus, from beavertail opuntia to at least six types of cholla to hedgehog, fishhook, and barrel, as well as Mojave yucca and desert agave. Each displayed its flowers. They could be fuchsia, gold, orange, tomato red, light yellow, beige, white, or green, all that insects happily swarmed to. It was inspiring, meditatively Zen-like, making us feel at one with Nature.

And taking the Palm Springs Aerial Tram was exciting. The ten-minute, two and one-half-mile trip took us from the hard-packed, baking desert floor on the north edge of Palm Springs to the 8,643-foot top of Mt. San Jacinto. Snowy and thirty degrees cooler, its forested wilderness briskly embraced us. All around were spectacular, breathtaking views. The experience was likewise spiritual.

Yes, Southern California still called to me. It was the ever-lurking appeal and aspiration, the golden desire for *what-could-be.* Maybe Faust and I could take a trip there. However, I knew that instead of finding that alluring, resplendent fantasy, we would merely come face-to-face with the harsh reality of 1980s' Southern California.

Since I had been there, there had been a housing super-explosion. Nearly any available piece of land had been converted to residential developments. Commercial sprawl dominated with block-after-block of one-level, concrete-building-dotted strip malls, teeming with flashing neon and large signs. The significantly-increased, accompanying population had spawned all-day-and-all-night, stress-filled, slow-moving, bumper-to-bumper traffic. And smog was an ever greater issue. Even when we had visited the Anza-Borrego in 1969 and 1970, we could see the brown haze working its way from Los Angeles toward the desert.

Still, maybe a trip could help me more easily re-examine the benefits of living in the slightly less hectic, still-green, suburban Boston area. Of course, in Massachusetts there wouldn't be any Anza-Borrego Desert or Palm Springs Aerial Tramway, which Faust would have loved. But, at least, I knew in my carved-out section of the northeast there would be fewer dense marine fog banks, earthquakes, and town-surrounding, raging wildfires. Surely there was something to be said for that.

Yet, the more I thought about a trip to Southern California the more excited I became. But there was one big obstacle. Tom and Molly wanted their house back soon and Faust and I currently had no place else to go. If we were going anywhere on a trip, we had to have a residence to which to return.

20

A CASE OF CARPE DIEM

Something sort of off-the-wall occurred to me. What if I could take Harriet up on her Wellesley house? Rent it for a year? I didn't really want it but it might still be available and I needed it. But even as a rental, the house needed some fundamental work so it wouldn't be a heating money pit. Consequently, I decided if it were available, I'd rent it but only with the proviso that the owners would:

1. Install Fiberglass insulation, R-15, in the basement and garage between joists and in the attic between rafters.

2. Sweep the chimney, live-trap any critters at home there, and install a mesh chimney cap to keep out raccoons, squirrels, bats, owls, and swifts so I could use the fireplace as an additional heat source.

3. Fumigate the whole house for mice, remove rodent bodies, and clean out mice nests and droppings.

4. Pass a home inspection, one I'd pay for. I wanted to know what environmental problems I would be living with. For example, if the house were sitting on a rock ledge emitting copious amounts of radon or had a mold problem.

I could hire a neighborhood youngster to take care of cutting the lawn. The sixty-year-old house wasn't ideal—that was an understatement—but I needed to act quickly on something. We had had zero success finding anything remotely close to acceptable. Too often when the space was close to being right, the rent wasn't or the location or the state of disrepair was the pits. I was feeling desperate but I didn't want to take just anything to have a place called "home."

Even with the addition of insulation, to save on heating bills I would use the fireplace, determine if turning the heat down low in the rooms I didn't use and closing those doors, as well as adding heavy drapes, would help. That meant I needed to check on thermostat locations to see what was possible. In the old house there might be only one per floor.

Harriet was surprised, and perhaps not thrilled, to hear from me again. But when I explained that I was possibly interested in her listing off Weston Road if it were still on the market, she became very friendly. Straightaway, we were like old school chums greeting at a reunion. Perhaps not unexpectedly the odd little house was still available. We made a quick-and-dirty appointment to see it, to arrive in separate cars. I decided to leave Faust in Sudbury. I could get through it much faster without him searching for mice and annoying Harriet. He would not be pleased and would make sure I knew about it when I returned.

After I left, it occurred to me that the load of

laundry I had done that morning was sitting in a basket in the bathroom, and an open invitation for Faust to vigorously roll around in it, coating every square inch of my underwear, towels, and unfolded sheets with gray fur. Definitely "too soon old and too late smart."

I had made up a list of every single thing I wanted to check before sharing with Harriet my requirements for renting. I figured that since the house had been available for a long time, the owners might be reasonable and more likely to accede to my very basic wishes. After all, I could represent their unloading this property eventually.

I wanted to sign a rental agreement with the attached written proviso that the insulation, chimney work, fumigation, and inspection would be done and done before I moved in. Harriet vetoed that. She said she would run it past the owners and would give me a call with their answer.

When I arrived home in Sudbury, I found Faust in the kitchen, dramatically hanging by his front paws from the refrigerator door handle. When he saw me, he didn't release it to run to greet me as he usually did. He was letting me know he was ticked off. Instead, he turned back toward the refrigerator. Using his back feet against the front side of the refrigerator, he pushed. The door seal hissed and the door swung open slightly. He let go of the handle, landed silently, and pushed his way into the appliance. He was not on a hunting expedition. He knew precisely what he wanted.

On the lower shelf was his aluminum-foil-covered cat food can. Grabbing it, he pulled it out and let it slide onto the linoleum. Then he casually clawed off the foil and began nibbling the food. The way he kept flicking his tongue as he sat attempting to eat suggested the frosty food was anything but palatable. But he was making a point. So he'd pretend until he was sure I got the message.

"Faust," I apologized, "I'm sorry I couldn't take you with me." Then, as I petted him, I launched into a life instruction he was sure to cover with mental cat litter. "Opening the refrigerator is not a good thing to do." He cocked his head to the right and looked at me as if barely tolerating this boring human tendency to lecture. "You might have gotten caught inside. Besides, the food isn't all that flavorful when it's cold and it will probably give you a tummy ache." He scanned my expression, angled away from me, lifted his right rear leg, doubled over, and commenced licking his nether regions. "How about we talk about this on the sofa?"

I closed the refrigerator door. He stopped his tongue movement, didn't look convinced, but insouciantly pushed the can aside to amble behind me into the living room. I put him on my lap and scratched a special location between the shoulder blades. Instantly, he raised his whiskers and began rapidly lapping the air and kneading my thighs. When I switched to scratching another such place above his tail, he lapped some more and hopped from one rear foot to other.

After my triggering two of his pleasure centers, he seemed reconciled to forgiving me. A soft-pawed rap to my nose, however, reminded me I was going to be on semi-probation for a while. If I played my cards right, another such extended special petting session would grease the skids for my receiving a quick presidential pardon.

Harriet called to say the owners of the house were less than pleased, not wanting to put any extra money into this property unless it were being sold. But they would consider it. Harriet said she didn't think it was very promising. That left Faust and me up in the air. Time was running out. Tom and Molly would be back very soon and we had no place to go.

Then it occurred to me. What if, since we had to pack a U-Haul with all our furniture anyway to move to wherever, we made our destination Southern California. Mother and I had done it before. Of course, we had had a clear-cut destination in mind then. However, the Rabbit, unlike the Sherman-tank-built Ford, couldn't pull the size U-Haul trailer we'd need. That meant we'd have to rent a 45-mph-max, small truck and tow the car.

As I still carefully scanned the "Houses for Rent" section for the next several days and checked out two Open Houses, it was obvious we weren't securing a rental in the area any time soon.

Because the Sudbury house had been furnished, I had had to get rid of some of what I had brought with me, items that I couldn't fit into the second bedroom as storage. There was no room in the small, one-car garage for anything but the car, the bicycle, and some tools. Besides I worried about the possibility of water damage, insects, mice infestation, and mold there.

What I had left were a double-bed (mattress, box spring, and fruitwood bed frame with headboard), one-drawer fruitwood nightstand, nightstand lamp, five-drawer fruitwood clothes dresser, a round maple kitchen table with two matching chairs, a steel four-shelf bookcase, a gray government steel desk, a rolling chair, a modern-looking three-seater sofa in a deep brown, rough-textured fabric with foam-filled cushions on wooden legs, numerous cardboard cartons of books, vinyl records, bed linen and towels, pots, pans, and dishware, seasonal clothing, an IBM Selectric typewriter,17-inch Panasonic CRT television, Technics turntable with clear plastic cover, and two very small KLH speakers. All this filled the ten-by-ten room. As I thought about it, I now wished I hadn't gotten rid of my other stuff. Maybe I could have tried harder to wedge it in … somehow.

Because we were financially-stretched, I wanted to supplement this with some less expensive pieces of furniture we still needed no matter where we moved. If we did go to California, I didn't want to have to search for furniture once we were there. Decent but cheaper was the goal. With an itemized list in hand, we headed down to closeout store, a huge warehouse called "Building #19" on Route 9 in

Natick. Their fun motto was "Good Stuff ... Cheap!"

If you knew what to look for, you could find some great bargains. In the past I had found brand-name sweat shirts, leather knee-high boots, and a handsome, new—tags still attached—Ivy League-style, wool and polyester sports jacket from Brooks Brothers, with navy, gray, and terra cotta threads. It fitted as if it had been custom-tailored for me. I wore that beautiful blazer for the next ten years. That is, until moth-ball-huffing, mutant mega-moths invaded the garment bag and pigged out on the back of the jacket. Nature can be cruel.

Much of Building #19's eclectic merchandise was overstock, factory irregulars, discontinued models, customs' seizures, liquidations, damaged or less-than-perfect, and new merchandise as well. Occasionally you'd smell those that resulted from a *real* "fire sale." Exploring there was like being on a treasure hunt. As much as I hated to shop—I mean, I *really* hated to shop—when I absolutely, positively needed some specific piece of casual clothing or furniture, this was the place to check first before I hit Shopper's World in Framingham.

When we arrived, we were immediately confronted by store "security personnel." Dressed in a navy blue shirt that strained its buttons to cover a beer gut which hung over low-slung navy pants, he was a short, in his late thirties, with a blond military crew-cut. Imperiously, he pointed at Faust lounging around my neck. "And what's this, sweetheart?"

Annoyed, but assuming a wide-eyed look of innocence, I said, "I'm looking for a cat carrier that he needs to try on so I can be assured of a proper fit."

He rolled his eyes and shook his head, "That's cute." After a moment, he looked me up and down, raised an eyebrow, and smiled wickedly. "Okay, sweetheart, you just go on ahead. But I'm going to keep an eye on you. You'll be sure to let me know if I can give you a hand, won't you," he snickered with a wink.

Yeah, sure, "sweetheart," I thought, you can count on it. As much as I felt the urge to put my finger down my throat, I let it go. We had managed to pass muster and needed to get on with what we came to do. With all the inviting sights and sounds of this busy warehouse, I beseeched the fates that Faust wouldn't create a problem. While it wasn't likely this well-mannered feline would, it wasn't beyond the realm of possibility that he might decide to caterwaul along with the piped in strains of Muzak, sharpen his claws on a smoky-smelling fabric of an overstuffed chair, or whizz on some highly ornate, gilded ceramic items he considered kitsch. Everyone is a critic.

On the ceiling between the metal rafters were hung oak-and-brass fans which rotated slowly and silently, keeping the temperature from all the circulating bodies below comfortable. Faust and I would spend less than an hour browsing and inspecting. But not straying from my list wasn't easy. For all I knew, there might be another splendiferous sports jacket calling to me. As it quickly turned out, history did not repeat itself.

This particular day there was a lot of furniture to examine. The array covered living and dining rooms as well as kitchens and bedrooms. I found two wrought iron floor lamps, two metal table lamps, an un-named wood television cart with a lower shelf for my turntable, a contemporary accent club chair, and a slatted fruitwood coffee table all of which I tagged to pick up later. I was contemplating getting several area rugs in case we found ourselves with uncarpeted floors, like in Wellesley, but maybe that should wait until we actually found a place. Still, I reflected, it wouldn't hurt to look.

The rug section was like an invitation into a Middle-Eastern bazaar. Larger rugs, at least six-foot-by-twelve-foot, were hanging on hooks on movable arms jutting out from the building's right-side wall. Some rugs looked Persian or so-called "oriental," some had floral or geometric designs, others were monotone. There were shag, short-pile, and sculpted rugs in cotton, polyester, or wool. They were in behind the raised platform on which the smaller unrolled rugs were displayed. I was looking particularly for four-by-six wool shag rugs in abstract patterns of some combination of orange, red, yellow, black or tan.

As I was leaning over, flipping corners of the flattened rugs aside to see what they had, Faust jumped from my shoulders. At that moment I hadn't realized that his leash was not wrapped tightly around my right wrist as usual. Suddenly I heard strange scraping sounds behind me. Faust was nowhere in sight. I turned to look in the sound's direction. To my horror Faust's leash was sticking out the end of the four-inch-diameter, twelve-foot-long cardboard rug tube someone had left lying on the floor behind the hanging rugs. Involuntarily my hand covered my mouth as I gasped. What the ...? Oh crap!

Faust was small but not small enough to squeeze on through. I had no idea how he had progressed as far as he had. Even though cats have free-floating clavicle bones, instead of rigid shoulders, and can compress themselves into tight places, this time it was not going to work. Not in a four-inch diameter, especially with him wearing a harness. Undoubtedly realizing he was not moving forward, he tried to scramble out backwards. But attempting to use his back feet raised his haunches, snugging him in even more tightly.

Racing to the tube, I tried pulling him by his leash. That didn't work. He didn't budge. I should have known better. Cats don't like to be pulled on. They'll invariably freeze in place or, if they can, try to move in the opposite direction. He had managed to crawl in just far enough that I couldn't grab his back legs because they were buried under him. Moreover, oddly enough, his tail was wedged beside him, making everything even tighter. I was not going to be able to drag him out. Last-ditch ideas flitted past, one after another, and faded away.

I asked myself if I had my utility knife with me. I usually carried a thin orange plastic-covered razor knife in my handbag. You just never knew when it would come in handy. But using it would have been dangerous ... potentially cutting into Faust's flesh if the knife slipped on the slick cardboard surface, or if I misjudged his position inside, or if he moved somehow. Maybe a saw would work? No, it was the same problem. Besides, I didn't want to alert store personnel to Faust's predicament if I could help it.

It seemed like hours, but was only a matter of seconds. Then something possibly more helpful occurred to me. Standing behind the hanging rugs, I hoisted the long tube into the air. With the leash-end down, I awkwardly raised the tube to vertical. The opening was just five inches above the floor. As I struggled to keep the top from swaying, shifting the tube direction, I could hear movement.

Physics was on our side. Rhythmically I shook the tube up and down. Slowly Faust oozed out, inch by furry inch. He was still in the process of attempting to scratch hold of the smooth inner surface with his front claws as he unceremoniously plopped out, his bottom thumping on the floor. Gravity had saved us.

Quickly I looked around. No one was gawking in our direction or running toward the rug section, firearms drawn. I decided against further rug contemplation. With Faust back on my shoulders, his belly hugging the back of my neck, and his leash wrapped several times around my wrist, I hurried to a register ... red-faced but relieved.

After I paid for our selections, I had the tagged lamps, TV cart, accent chair, and coffee table taken to the loading dock. I pulled the Rabbit around, opened the hatch and flattened the rear seats to accommodate our purchases. Fortunately by pushing the front passenger-side seat back to provide more leg room and lowering its seatback, I could position the accent chair there. That meant I didn't need to leave the hatch open and rope everything into place.

An open hatch would have been impossible for Faust to resist. In retrospect, I could picture him as "Andy," Rollie Tyler's assistant in *F/X*, where she had strapped herself in standing at the open back of the F/X van as it charged around New York City streets. Faust would have loved it.

Over time, if necessary, I could replace some of these items with more permanent pieces. But as long as they functioned as needed, more or less matched, and looked acceptable, I didn't care. I wasn't interested in duplicating interior decoration schemes from *Town and Country Magazine*. For now we'd have the essentials for a small house. The next thing on our agenda was for Faust and me to start making plans for our California road trip—first of all deciding our precise destination.

When Harriet called again, I assumed she had the "bad" news that the Wellesley house owners wouldn't budge. I was ready to grin and bear it because Faust and I had already begun discussing our next big adventure. But people can surprise you when you least expect it. To my amazement she said that while the owners were still disgruntled about having to insulate and fumigate the house, particularly within two weeks, they would accede to my requests as long as I signed the rental for a minimum of three years, though longer would be better. Furthermore, they hoped I'd consider buying after renting. It was a go after all.

I was torn. Their not wanting to insulate and fumigate the house—a house I really didn't want in the first place—had given me the excuse to allow myself to follow a whim, to pick up, and head west. But rationally, I had to admit that zipping off to Southern California was not the most pragmatic or advantageous action for me to take right now. I was making progress establishing myself as a coach and seminar provider. I had speaking gigs signed up with local groups, like the Rotary. I had another book in the works for my publisher, Brick House. Moreover, I had developed a proposal for a half-hour educational program on alternative career development I wanted to submit to the local community cable station.

At the same time, I didn't want to lock myself into staying there three years. If this were a house I wanted to eventually buy, then maybe. But I had no idea what the house would be like, if it would gobble up my bank account as I tried to stay warm in the winter even with the added insulation and working fireplace. Maybe within the year the housing market would improve and I could find something I really wanted to rent, or even buy. At the moment we didn't have a whole lot of choice.

In the back of my mind California still glittered before me like a phantasm of the unattainable, like the Maltese Falcon, in the film of the same name, "the things that dreams are made of." Faust and I would definitely go, at least for a trip. I definitely wanted us to check out Death Valley, maybe even camp. In the meantime, I had to inform Harriet of our acquiescence, schedule the house inspection for when the work was done, rent a small U-Haul truck with a car trailer, get some help packing the truck, and move us.

Resigned, I gathered Faust into my arms and danced around the living room, singing to the tune of "Happy Days are Here Again."

"We finally have a place to stay
With grass and trees for you to play.
But no more little gray and furry prey.
Our new life episode starts today."

It really wasn't working out all that badly, I consoled myself. We'd be settled, with a home base. I'd submit my cable-program proposal and continue to work on my next book where I could easily meet with the publisher for conferences. I'd somehow figure out something for meeting with clients. There would be more time to plan for checking out the Golden State.

Faust and I would finally have our much-anticipated, rejuvenating, cross-country odyssey, like Art Carney and his beloved marmalade cat in the film *Harry and Tonto*, which showed there's simply nothing as life-affirming as having a cat as your wheel man. Whaaa-hooo!

ABOUT THE AUTHOR

Signe A. Dayhoff, PhD, is a social psychologist with post-graduate training in counseling who received her doctorate from Boston University. There she worked on ways to improve job and career advancement through networking relationships and mentoring. For over 34 years she has been a cognitive-behaviorist, coach, and author in the areas of education-based relationship marketing, interpersonal communications, and social effectiveness. She specializes in overcoming obstacles, eliminating limiting beliefs, maximizing skills and confidence, and alleviating social anxiety.

An applied feline behaviorist and rescuer, she is currently kitty-mom to 18 senior, chronically ill, and disabled cats. She consults on improving human-cat relationships from both the human and cat's communication perspective and advocates for the adoption of homeless animals.

She has taught psychology at Boston University, University of Massachusetts, and Framingham State College and has done research at Massachusetts Institute of Technology, Scripps Clinic and Research Foundation, and Fairview State Hospital.

She is author of thirteen other books, including *Remarkable Tales of Cats Who Whisper to Humans*;

How Intrepid the Disabled Kitten Triumphed to Help Others; *What Faust the Dancing Cat Taught Me*; *Attracting and Dating the Wrong Men: Tips and Insights to Free Yourself*; *Growing Up "Unacceptable"—How Katharine Hepburn Rescued Me*; *What No One Has Told You: How Insiders Really Get Jobs*; *Scared of Your Boss? Smash Through Your Fear Now*; *Promote Myself? I'd Rather Eat Worms!*; *How to Speak Without Fear Small Talk Course*; the 2nd Ed. of *Diagonally-Parked in a Parallel Universe: Working Through Social Anxiety* (the social phobic's bible and insider's scoop, which has been praised by noted clinical researchers); *Create Your Own Career Opportunities*; *Get The Job You Want*; and *Decision Making For Managers.* She has contributed to David Riklan's *101 Great Ways to Improve Your Life (Vol. 2)*; Steven J. Bennett's *Executive Chess: Creative Problem Solving By 45 of America's Top Business Leaders and Thinkers*; and *How to Reduce Your Anxiety Through Nutrition* with Dr. Elizabeth Lipski. She has made presentations nationally on social anxiety, social effectiveness, mentoring, and the human-animal bond.

Be sure to check out her website at http://effectivenessplus.com